One Minute Miracles

BRINGING YOU
ONE
MINUTE
MIRACLES

Ignite 52 Religious Truths to
Set You Free and Bring Peace

CLAUDIA T. NELSON

NEW YORK

LONDON • NASHVILLE • MELBOURNE • VANCOUVER

One Minute Miracles

Ignite 52 Religious Truths that Set You Free and Bring You Peace of Mind

Published in New York, New York, by Morgan James Publishing. Morgan James is a trademark of Morgan James, LLC. www.MorganJamesPublishing.com

Proudly distributed by Publishers Group West®.

Morgan James BOGO™

A **FREE** ebook edition is available for you or a friend with the purchase of this print book.

CLEARLY SIGN YOUR NAME ABOVE

Instructions to claim your free ebook edition:
1. Visit MorganJamesBOGO.com
2. Sign your name CLEARLY in the space above
3. Complete the form and submit a photo of this entire page
4. You or your friend can download the ebook to your preferred device

ISBN 9781636980843 paperback
ISBN 9781636980850 ebook
Library of Congress Control Number:
2022948325

Cover Design by:
Rachel Lopez
www.r2cdesign.com

Cover Image Produced by:
Lyle Friedman

Morgan James PUBLISHING Builds with... Habitat for Humanity Peninsula and Greater Williamsburg

Morgan James is a proud partner of Habitat for Humanity Peninsula and Greater Williamsburg. Partners in building since 2006.

Get involved today! Visit: www.morgan-james-publishing.com/giving-back

ALSO BY CLAUDIA NELSON

Murder, Death and Rebirth
Rising from Ashes: Discover Your Hidden Power through Adversity
The Hero's Journey: A Visual Journey of Spiritual Transformation
Ellie's Magical Unicorn
Maggie's Not so Cocky Peacock

This book is dedicated to Ronald Lee Brown,
whose generosity made it possible for this book to be in your hands.

In discussing this book before he passed, Ron wanted me to remind you
that you have all knowledge and all answers hidden inside yourself.
This book does not attempt to give you all the answers;
it gives you tools to remove the blocks, or veils, standing
between you and your own answers and provides the keys
to opening the secret doors where all knowledge is hidden.

ART WORK

The late Jerry Jampolsky, M.D. and his wife Diane Cirincione, Ph.D. graciously allowed me to use illustrations from Jerry's bestselling book, *Love is Letting Go of Fear*, to help illustrate *One-Minute Miracles*. With Jerry's passing, Diane is now executive director of Attitudinal Healing International. It is a wonderful personal and community resource. Additional art concepts were created by B. Smith—from which Stephanie Mullani created additional art. Each image was created to blend with the Jampolsky art, to assure there was an illustration to enhance each of the fifty-two lessons.

ONE OF THE MOST CHALLENGING AND REWARDING
THINGS YOU CAN EVER DO IS CHANGE YOUR THINKING,

TO SEE THINGS DIFFERENTLY.

WHEN YOU DO . . .

MIRACLES HAPPEN.

WELCOME TO THE BOOK THAT SHOWS YOU HOW!

TABLE OF CONTENTS

WHY I WROTE
ONE-MINUTE MIRACLES

The information in *One-Minute Miracles* came from a blog written nearly a decade ago, called *Monday Morning Tips.*

It was amazing to have thousands of thank you messages come back from countries all over the world; the remarks like, *finally something useful*, were followed by many exclamation marks!!

Being focused on caring for my husband's health issues, I neglected the blog, and after time it disappeared. After his death I got a spiritual download that the information needed to be put into a book. This book was partially written before an accident crushed my L1 vertebra.

Two and a half years later, having recovered from the injury, I find my own country, and much of the known world, in chaos and fear being engulfed in a war between good and evil. It was now clear why I got the download. One-Minute Miracles is here to help make sense of our times—to answer the question we are all asking . . . why is our old world, and personal worlds, as we have known them, breaking down? And how are we going to get through it and remain mentally intact?

One-Minute Miracles will help you understand why we are experiencing all the chaos in the world, and it is all good in the end. The world and its people are going through a much-needed cleanse. The purpose is to clean things up to make way for a wonderful new age. So, hang in there. It is all good.

One-Minute Miracles will not only help you understand the chaos and survive it, it will help you thrive through it.

As you progress through the lessons, you will come to have a clearer understanding of the chaos and its specific purposes. You will become increasingly peaceful as you navigate through the lessons and will eventually be grateful for the fear and chaos that helped bring you to this understanding and peace.

Tesla and Einstein give us a clue as to where many of these peace bringing answers are found.

*"The day science begins to study non-physical phenomena,
it will make more progress in one decade than in all the
previous centuries of existence."*
(Nikola Tesla)

*You can't solve your problems at the same level of thinking
you were at when you created them."*
(Albert Einstein)

WHY READ
ONE-MINUTE MIRACLES

What do we all desire? Is it not the freedom to love and be loved and find peace of mind? How then do we find the freedom to accomplish that? The answer is found in John 8:32, where we read: "Ye shall know the Truth and the truth shall set you free." Here is one truth Jesus the Christ gives us that can help set us free. He said:

"If you do NOT bring forth what is within you, what is within you will destroy you. If you bring forth what is within you, what is within in you will save you."

Based on my experience, this passage from the Gospel of Thomas, recovered from the Dead Sea Scrolls, is brilliant. But, when discovered in the last century, it was quite controversial. This is understandable because it was not understood at that time.

Yet, we now find it again in *The Way of Mastery,* a book which is designed to reintroduce and clarify Christ's teachings, including this one. Yes, Christ is speaking to us again.

The above quote may seem confusing. From my perspective, based on research as well as experience, this quote is simply saying you have two things within you and one of these things needs to come forth to save you and the other needs to eliminated to keep it from destroying you.

He has revealed what will save you . . .

> "If you do not bring forth what is within in you—AND WHAT IS WITHIN YOU IS LOVE . . . you will feel burdened and unfulfilled, usually most human beings go through their entire life with a sense of lack of fulfillment, lamenting what the world has done to them, lamenting the decisions and choices they have made in the past. They become burdened by what is on the outside, along with what is past. And eventually the body dies, the Spirit withers on the vine." (*The Way of Mastery*)

It is not so clear what it is within you that must be brought forth that *destroys* you. However, my experience, my observation, and my research validates what *The Way of Mastery* teaches. *It teaches that it is—* our FEARS, **hidden** within, that destroy.

> **"God hath not given us a spirit of fear but of power,**
> **and of love, and of a sound mind"**
> **(2 Timothy 1:7).**

How do we discover these fears within us that destroy? We move to a different level of thinking as Einstein suggests. There we discover our fears so we can eliminate them as well as finding our power, love and our sound mind. So how do we do that? That is the purpose of this book, "Be ye transformed by the renewing of your mind" (Romans 12:2).

WHAT TO EXPECT FROM *ONE-MINUTE MIRACLES*

This book may call on your courage to challenge your old ways of thinking. But . . . if you will hang in there with an open mind and work the simple one-minute lessons, you will be so happy you did, as it will ultimately open your eyes to a much happier and more peaceful way of living. You will know the Truth and the "Truth will set you free."

To assist you in digesting important, but essential concepts and principles some of which may be unfamiliar to you, they will be repeated at different times in slightly different ways. We learn by repetition.

On my own reprogramming journey, I learned the most effective way to reprogram was to look at life from many perspectives and through the eyes of those who saw things differently. This method came to me in a very profound dream. Later, this concept was validated when studying the life of famous psychiatrist, Dr. Carl Jung.

Taking what I felt credible from each perspective, then connecting the dots and with the help of meditation and a higher power, you have *One-Minute Miracles.*

This book is designed to bring you a simple program that will, when diligently followed, bring up, for healing, what is within you that will destroy you, as well as what is in you that will save you. Even one lesson can create miracles in your life.

Why is this important? Because the chaotic world we live in will never change until the people do; as this world is made of up people!

"Be ye transformed by the renewing of your mind"
(Romans 12:2).

INTRODUCTION

This book is designed to begin the process of correcting every misperception about yourself, your relationships and your world that has held you back from seeing your own magnificence. By living the simple step-by-step principles in this book, you will be astonished to see a transformation take place in your life as you discover the *real* you.

Now more than ever, we need to rediscover our own power and learn how to take it back in order to survive the chaos, trauma and change all around us.

One-Minute Miracles reveals the entrance to the door of your own creative powers, allowing you to open it, walk through it and discover:

1. *Your own phenomenal personal guidance system.*
2. *Your own creative powers.*
3. *How to use this power to* **consciously** *create what you truly desire.*
4. *The Truths you seek.*

You have always been a creator. Not being aware of this, you have been creating by default; creating situations you would not be seeking if you were creating consciously.

One-Minute Miracles explains your two thought systems, and how one creates seemingly randomly and often destructively, and the other creates positively and shows you how to get from your lower thought system to your higher thought system. Throughout the book, these two thought systems are referred to in different ways.

Generally, the positive healthy thought system will be referred to as our 99% thought system, as that is where we find 99% of truth. Occasionally, I may refer to it as our Spiritual Thought System, our Love-Based Thought System, our Big Self, our Higher Self, Smart Part, Source, or Force.

Generally, I will refer to our negative thought system as our 1% thought system as that is where we find only 1% of truth. Occasionally, I will refer to it as our Dumb Part, Lower Self, Little Self, Physical Self, Ego, or Fear-Based Thought System.

Our entire way of life is changing . . . our moral system, our political system, and our financial system, etc., causing global chaos. This can be very frightening if you don't understand what is happening or why.

Is that bad news?

No!

Because there is a personal and global transformation occurring which is creating beneficial results which are not yet visible, but will soon be understood.

According to Dr. Carl Jung, along with many metaphysical and spiritual teachings, this is part of a positive transformation occurring both personally and globally, which Dr. Jung calls *The Individuation Process.*

This process is a three-stage process. For our purpose here you need know only the first stage. The remaining two will be revealed in other lessons further along in this book.

This *Individuation Process* is the process by which we become emotionally and spiritually healthy, which begins with disintegration as will be further explained in the lesson section of this book.

Stage 1: Disintegration.

The old must disintegrate before the new can emerge, as you cannot put "new wine in old bottles" as the old spoils the new.

So, the bad news is not really bad at all. Darkness, opposition and chaos always show up when there is great change. The great change is that the corrupt energy is dying. This old abusive fear-based energy must die to make room for the new love-based energy to emerge. Yet it is dying hard; fighting for its life.

Die it must, for love and fear can't occupy the same space at the same time, just as two objects can't occupy the same space at the same time. And we are moving from a world of fear to a world of love.

Great evils have been practiced for centuries on our planet, but they have been hidden. Now they are being exposed. What we are learning is often shocking and traumatizing. Yet exposure is essential, for you can't heal what you can't see.

The good news is now that we can see the evils, they can be, and are being, eradicated or healed, making way for a wonderful new world of love to emerge. These difficult times are a catalyst for bringing about this new world through Dr. Jung's aforementioned *Individuation Process.*

Just as a builder needs tools to build a new house, we need tools to build a new life and a new world. As you read this book and commit to the simple daily practices, you will begin to understand why the world is now in the state it is and how you can help transform it without becoming an activist, unless being an activist is something you feel called to do.

It is my constant prayer and deepest desire that this information will help you navigate through the present chaos. May you not only survive, but thrive; may you emerge healthier and happier than you have ever been and KNOW that you are making a difference in this world while helping yourself just by changing your vibrational energy, which happens automatically as you practice these lessons.

The process you will be going through is validated by Dr. Bruce Lipton and the new cutting edge science of Epigenetics.

> **"We can create the world we want, and all we have to do is**
> _____.**"**
> **(Dr. Bruce Lipton)**

By the time you finish this book you will know how Dr. Lipton finished this sentence.

Applying the tools found in this small book will not only assist you in increasing your vibrational energy, you will begin learning the secrets of the universe about gaining and/or maintaining peace and happiness.

And you can become a lighthouse to keep others who are lost from crashing during the storm. Again, this is my prayer for you and those you will influence!

> **"If you want to find the secrets of the Universe,**
> **think in terms of energy, frequency and vibration."**
> **(Nikola Tesla)**

Don't feel bad if you don't understand this statement now. You will when you finish the book.

How I Know These Miracle Tips Can Transform Your Life

How do I know what you will experience when you diligently work these Miracle Tips? Because I have lived every one of them and experienced their results.

You see, I had been experiencing trauma after trauma until I became so depressed I couldn't find my way across the street and thought I had Alzheimer's.

Not so; it was a severe depression caused by my going off Prozac cold turkey. Prozac is an anti-depressant drug I had been taking for five years to handle the pain of the murders and the divorce I had experienced. The depression surfaced when I went off the medication.

The pain was so severe I have no judgment about anyone who commits suicide. What a relief death would have been. I couldn't do that because it would have been too traumatic for my children, so I had to find another way. What you find in *One-Minute Miracles* is the path to health, peace and happiness I found through my own healing journey.

Some of the traumas were so dramatic the media picked them up. CBS's *48 Hours, Live to Tell* picked up the story about the murder of my mother and sister ("Three Days Before Christmas") and PBS and *Forbes* magazine picked up the story of the Ponzi scheme in which I lost my life savings. Losing my brother to suicide, my father in a car wreck while I was on my honeymoon, my bout with cancer, and my divorce, never hit the media, but those events were every bit, or more, devastating than anything picked up by the media.

Later in life, I remarried and became a widow. While obviously painful, I knew better how to handle trauma and used what I had learned through previous traumas to get through this more gracefully. The point is, yes I know these Miracle Tips work because they worked to save me.

More details on the traumas I faced can be found in *Rising from Ashes: Discover your Hidden Power through Adversity*.

How to Get the Most from Your Miracle Tips

This book is meant to be experienced, not simply read like other books. Just thumb through it look at the Table of Contents, get a general overview, then read and work a couple of Miracle Tips. Seeing their value, you will want to:

Set Up Your Team

For maximum benefit, decide upon one to seven (1–7) people with whom you want to share and discuss each Miracle Tip. It can be a family member(s), neighbors, friends, or you can form a Miracle discussion group with the number you can comfortably engage.

- *It is a natural law of the universe that you must give to receive. As you are giving something valuable to them you are gaining value for yourself.*

Make a list of people you might want on your team. Contact those on the list and, explain your project. Read one of your favorite lessons to them, explain how it has helped you. Invite them to join you.

Once you have found those people who are interested in participating, set up one day of the week to talk to each committed individual at the same time each day. Limit each conversation to three to five minutes, unless you both have an abundance of time; otherwise, it will become difficult to continue. Remember, you eat an elephant one bite at a time.

On your first visit, if your friends don't have the book, read the lesson and the assignment both of you will work on for the week. Discuss your progress and experience the second week. Then, read them the next Miracle Tip you will discuss the following week and end the call. Continue this pattern each week, progressively working through the Miracle Tips.

There will likely come a time when you will begin to engage in profound discussions that will become more important than anything else, and your time for discussion will increase. This is wonderful as it is a sign you are beginning to see these lessons change your life.

Suggest to each team member they "Pay it Forward" and start their own Miracle group when they finish yours, or continue as a group for a while if you prefer. The more you and they give and share, the more you and they get out of each lesson. Each Miracle Tip will then be yours and *theirs* to keep and use to more easily transform their lives.

This may seem like a small thing; however, with a little discipline you will reap big benefits. Altering thinking patterns is a miracle and a huge part of transformation. Take it seriously, for out of seemingly small things great things come to pass.

Personal Preparation

The following suggestions are a gift from the late adult and child psychiatrist Gerald Jampolsky, M.D., who understands how the mind works best:

- Beginning with One-Minute Miracles, Tip 1, practice the lessons sequentially . . . One tip every day for a week.
- Every day on awakening, relax and use your active imagination. In your mind's eye, put yourself somewhere you will feel comfortable, relaxed and at peace. Read the One-Minute Miracles tip.

- Spend a few minutes while you are in this relaxed state repeating the lesson title and related thoughts several times, allowing them to become part of your being. After this practice would be an optimal time for your three to five minute conversation with each of your group.
- Each day ask yourself the question, "Do I want to experience PEACE OF MIND or do I want to experience CONFLICT?"
- Put the lesson title for the week on a card and keep it with you. Review it periodically throughout the day and evening, and apply the lesson to everyone and everything without exception.
- Before retiring, relax and take a few minutes to review the day's lesson. Ask yourself if you are willing to have these ideas incorporated in your dreams.
- When you have considered all of the lessons, your learning will be further facilitated if you begin again with Miracle 1 and repeat all 52 miracles.
- **Lessons.** This book is called *One-Minute Miracles* for a reason. If you practice these tips, you will create miracles in your life.
- This form of practice is most helpful if it is maintained until you are thinking about the lessons and applying them consistently without needing to refer to them.

Assignment

Purchase a pack of 3x5 cards. Set up your *One-Minute Miracle* group and the day and time you will speak to each person, preferably at the same time every day.

SECTION ONE:
THE MIRACLES

MIRACLE TIP | WEEK ONE
THE WORLDS WE LIVE IN

"... there is a curtain that divides our reality into two
realms ... the 1% and the 99%. The 1% encompasses
our physical world, but this is only a tiny fraction of all
Creation. It is only what we perceive with our five senses ..."
[seeing, hearing, smelling, tasting and touching]
(Yehuda Berg, Kabbalist)

Note well the quote! We will be using these numbers to designate which thought system we are referring to throughout the book. **We call the ego-based world of fear thoughts the 1% world, for there you find only 1% of truth.** This world of thought is often called the Lower Self, Little Self, Physical Self, Dumb Part, Ego or Fear-Based Self.

We call the spiritual world of love the 99% world, for that is where you find 99% of truth. This world of thought is often called the Higher Self, Big Self, Non-Physical Self, Smart Part, Source, Force, or Love-Based self, or God self,

The yin/yang symbol symbolizes the opposites in all things. This illustration represents our opposing worlds, including our world of darkness and light.

Is the life you are living the kind of life you want? Or, do you feel like a caterpillar, living in survival mode whose great goal in life is to find its next leafy meal? Do you feel . . .

- Confused?
- That you are more often reactive than proactive?
- Victimized by others and external circumstances?
- That the majority of your desires remain unfulfilled?
- Fear of not having enough or not being enough?

This is the tragic truth for most of us; particularly now. This Covid world as thrown us deeper into the 1% **fear-based** world of confusion, darkness and chaos.

Carl Jung, and others, tell us: *Every negative thought or action is fear-based when reduced to its lowest common denominator*

Also, remember that, "You can't solve your problems at the same level of thinking you were at when you created them." (Albert Einstein)

You created your problems in your 1% world of thought. Next week, we will be discussing the 99% world. Where we solve them.

"He who looks outside dreams, he who looks inside awakens."
(Dr. Carl Gustav Jung)

Assignment

Write the following sentence on a 3x5 card and recite the following 25 times a day, either internally or out loud, every day this week. Continue thinking this: *I desire to exit this 1% world of fear. I will do whatever it takes to help it happen.*

MIRACLE TIP | WEEK TWO

THE PLACE YOU WANT TO BE: A SNEAK PREVIEW OF THE 99% WORLD

The Stupa, originally built to house relics of the Buddha,
or his disciples, came to be used as a symbol. The square base represents
earth, the circle water, the triangle fire, the semicircle air, and
the flame ether. Energy flows upward through these decreasingly
dense levels of matter until it transforms into spirituality.

*"What lies before us and what lies behind us are small
matters compared to what lies within us. And when we bring
what is in us out into the world miracles happen."*
(Ralph Waldo Emerson)

"If you want to find the secrets of the Universe think in terms of energy, frequency and vibration," says Nikola Tesla. The 99% world lies within. It is a place of a higher energy, higher frequency and higher vibration; a place of less dense matter that Buddhists call spirituality, the place where 99% of truth is found. The purpose of these *One-Minute Miracles* is to show you, in a simple step by step way, how to find, and connect to, this world.

But . . . what is this world like?

While the world of our Smart Part, where our Higher Self lives, lies beyond what you can perceive with your five senses, here is a sneak preview of that world. It is a world of . . .

- Smart thinking
- Light, order, perfection, and LOVE
- No victims, no victimizers, and . . . NO FEAR
- Those who are proactive and take responsibility for their lives
- Fulfillment, knowledge and endless joy
- Creation; the place we create our desires which manifest in the physical world

If it all sounds awesome and a bit intimidating; it is not. If it does, It is only because we have been **mis**-programmed, which you can reverse using these Miracle Tips.

Assignment

Write the following on a 3x5 card and read it several times a day, and keep thinking it: *I am excited to know of this 99% world. I am going to do all I can to gain access to it.*

MIRACLE TIP | WEEK THREE
EXPERIENCING THE TWO WORLDS

"Thoughts are things; they have tremendous power. Thoughts of doubt and fear are pathways to failure. When you conquer negative attitudes of doubt and fear, you conquer failure."
(Bryan Adams)

Now that you understand a bit about each world, the following experiment will help you experience the difference. For this experiment you will need:

- A watch with a second hand
- A yard, park, street or gymnasium
- One other person to help with the experiment
- The ability to run or walk approximately twenty or more yards—twice

First Run: Begin by having the participant spend at least seventeen seconds thinking of a very happy time and feeling it. Begin the run by having them continually say love over and over and feeling it. Time the run.

Second Run: Now have the participant spend at least seventeen seconds thinking of one of the worst, most miserable times of their life and feeling it. Have them say the word hate over and over as they are running, and feel it. Time that run.

Notice: How much faster did they run the first time? Their love thoughts gave them power, and a taste of the 99% world. Their anger thoughts kept them in the 1% world. They slowed them down, sapped their strength and robbed them of their power.

This experiment helps you begin to *experience* the difference between the two worlds—an experience that shows you one small benefit of connecting to your 99% Smart Part.

Assignment

This week, be continually aware of your feelings. They are your barometer of what you are thinking. They let you know if you are thinking 99% or 1% thoughts. Notice the 1% thoughts, say delete, and fill the vacuum with a 99% thought.

MIRACLE TIP | WEEK FOUR
YOUR THOUGHTS CREATE YOUR WORLD

"An unexamined life is not worth living."
(Socrates)

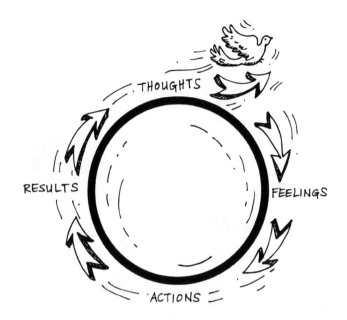

Explanation of Thought Wheel

- Thoughts put creative energy into motion (e-motion)
- Some energy goes into what Carl Jung, M.D., calls the "collective unconscious"
- Some energy goes into our body, creating our feelings
- Feelings move us to action
- Our actions create the results we are getting in life

It's that simple, but it takes effort to change our thinking. First you must make an honest examination of what you are truly thinking so you know what thinking needs to be corrected. Stay tuned to *One-Minute Miracles* to discover how.

Assignment

On another 3x5 card write this thought: *I examine my thoughts daily, hourly is even better, to see what they have created. I am willing to change those that no longer work.*

MIRACLE TIP | WEEK FIVE

CREATING THOUGHTS THAT ACCESS THE 99% WORLD

"It takes a lot of courage to release the familiar and seemingly secure, to embrace the new. But there is no real security in what is no longer meaningful . . . for in movement there is life, and in change there is power."
(Alan Cohen)

Last week, you learned how your thoughts create your world. Since you can't access your 99% world with 1% thinking, here are four ways to begin to replace confused 1% ego-based thoughts with our 99% Smart Part thoughts.

- Be willing to stop judging and begin to look at things differently—that means to give up your "I'm right, you're wrong" thinking.
- Be willing to stop blaming others and take responsibility for your life.
- Be willing to stop thinking about what you don't want or desire.
- Be willing to train your mind to think about what you do want or desire.

These four methods will challenge your ego-driven 1% thinking, your fear-based thought system. You can do it. You are in charge, not your ego. *Your ego is simply your fear-based thought system.*

"Heaven knows what price to place on its goods." This work will take some practice. This is good, as we place more value on things we have worked for. *One Minute Miracle's* tips will continue to support your efforts with added guidance with a meditation found in the appendix, with suggestions for further study at the end of the book, and more things on the drawing board to come later.

Assignment

Another mind monitoring week. Be the fly on the wall, observing yourself. Again, place the assignment on a notecard and read and act on it every day. Notice how many times a day you go into judging and other negative thinking. Don't judge yourself for it, just notice it.

MIRACLE TIP | WEEK SIX
HOW TO SEE THINGS DIFFERENTLY

"Through one-sidedness, the psyche disintegrates
and loses its capacity for cognition."
(Dr. Carl Jung)

Remember the story of the three blind men of Hindustan? Did you get the real moral?

Here's the story: One blind man stands by the elephant's tail, feels it and thinks it is a rope. Another standing by the leg, feels it, and thinks it is a tree. The third blind man standing by the trunk feels it and thinks it is a snake.

Were the men physically blind? Maybe. Or was it that they just couldn't see because they were standing too close, preventing them from seeing the big picture, the whole elephant, or the whole truth? They'd lost their capacity for cognition, or comprehension and discernment because of their one-sided, too close, or limited, view.

The lesson: The more views you see of something, the closer to truth you get.

You have a greater chance of seeing the big picture of anything if you look at it from a distance and/or from the perspectives of others as well as your own.

Looking through a keyhole never gives you an accurate picture of the whole house.

Assignment

Put your hand against your nose. What do you see? A blur? Move it two feet away. Look again. What do you see? Now you see clearly. Do this several times a day this week and remind yourself of this week's tip. Try to see one idea, or one experience, from a different angle every day, stand back, be objective and non-judgmental until you see clearly.

MIRACLE TIP | WEEK SEVEN
WHY FEAR IS SO DEADLY

"The only thing to fear is fear itself."
(Winston Churchill)

In light of the continued distressing news that our world seems to be falling apart, we will discuss fear. Fear is one of the major theses of OMM (*One-Minute Miracles*) and is discussed from several different angles. When seeing a new perspective that challenges your old one, never go into fear.

Don't do this: Don't go into fear no matter what. Why? Thoughts put energy into motion. Negative thoughts put negative energy into motion. Quantum Physics explains that negative thoughts connect to and create more negative thoughts, and eventually create more negative events.

Do this instead: Focus on a solution to your problem. Never focus on the problem again. Focusing on the problem keeps feeding the fear. Avoid focusing on the fear, even if something fearful is currently happening. Continue to focus on what you do want and the solutions that will get you there. Keep refining the solutions until they work.

Assignment

Observe your thoughts. You can shift yourself out of fear mode by following the instructions found under **"Do this instead"** above. It will be helpful for you to copy the instructions on a 3x5 card and look at it several times a day.

MIRACLE TIP | WEEK EIGHT

EFBD FORMULA
FOR DISSOLVING FEARS

"We can never obtain peace in the outer world
until we maintain peace within ourselves."
(Dali Lama)

When any negative experience or emotion escapes from your Pandora's box of emotional rocks . . . when reduced to its lowest common denominator, you will see that negative feelings and experiences are always generated by some kind of fear coming up for healing.

Our fears are created by our judgments. We recreate our judgments from the misinformation in our mental programs. Now is the time for healing. Everyone's "stuff" is coming up for healing in preparation for a whole new age of peace and prosperity. So, how does one heal, or neutralize, a fear?

Use the EFBD formula

1. **Embrace it.** Don't fight it or try to push it way. Ego would like you to judge it, ignore it or repress it again.
2. **Forgive it.** Seeing a situation differently helps you to forgive. This is magic. Forgiveness neutralizes the fear, helping you embrace it.
3. **Bless it.** Don't judge the fear, bless it. Blessing the fear dissolves the power it holds over you.

    Everything is only a learning experience and is neutral until we place a judgment on it.

4. **Dissolve it.** This happens automatically if you have successfully achieved Steps 1–3.

After you practice it for thirty days you will experience it for yourself. *Discover and eliminate your fears and **love** appears.* Without fear running your life, you will be able to create the life you desire even in this time of chaos. Perfect love does cast out fear. So, part of conquering fear is eventually coming to love it for the growth it has stimulated.

Assignment

Focus on one unresolved negative experience and practice using the EFBD Formula until the problem and your feelings are neutralized. If you are having a difficult time forgiving it, at least bless it for starters.

DISCOVERING OUR WANTS AND DESIRES

"The indispensable first step to getting things you want out of life is this: decide what you want [or desire]."
(Ben Stein)

Our **wants** are often difficult to identify because in the first three years of a child's life, he is told NO approximately 60,000 times—no, you can't have that—no, that will hurt you, or wanting that is selfish. So, he begins to fear his wants or feel guilty about them.

Another problem with understanding wants is that we don't understand the difference between wants and **desires.** Wants come from our lower, 1% self, and desires come from our 99% higher self. While it is preferable to live in our 99% thought system, our 1% wants are not wrong, for they often teach difficult, but valuable lessons. But these lessons are good, for they teach us we truly want to create from our 99% world.

As we mature spiritually, we come to understand that **desires are essential** for creating anything. As you mature through these *One-Minute Miracles* you will notice something interesting happening . . . you will recognize that you won't really want to create from your wants any longer. You will merely observe them; for creating from your 99% desires is what brings peace and happiness.

> *Never judge or fear your wants or desires.*
> *Be a fly on the wall and observe them.*

As you mature through these *One-Minute Miracles lessons,* if you're diligent in doing your assignments, you will be ready to separate your wants from your true desires and know how to create from your 99% thought system.

Assignment

As a want or desire emerges, begin practicing simply observing it. Try to determine which thought system it is coming from—your higher or lower thought system. Ask your higher self if this want or desire feeds the ego or the spirit. Ask what would be the long-term results if this want or desire were to manifest.

MIRACLE TIP | WEEK TEN
CREATING THINKING HABITS THAT EVOLVE US

"All the water in the ocean can't sink a ship unless it gets inside."
(Unknown)

Fear creates holes in our love boat. Let fear go, as the image suggests. Thinking with Love allows us to evolve.

Know This: Fear of judgment and criticism from others, and ourselves, keeps us stuck in old beliefs and sinks our boat full of love. The critic thinks his perception is THE truth, but it is only HIS truth—his perception. Unkind words come from fear. If we are not acting out of love, we are acting out of fear. Fear distorts truth.

Do this: Resist accepting another's negative opinion and going into the fear of "I'm not okay." Pretend you are producing a movie, and create your characters. These characters will replay a difficult scene from your life, but they will be neutral characters.. Become the observer and see how these characters handle this difficult situation in your life. Do they solve it for you? In the movie, do you see the situation, yourself and your answers more clearly?

You are writing the scene. You could write the scene the way you want it to play out where everyone comes out peaceful and happy. And you could keep editing the scene until it feels right. This is one creative way of discovering unique solutions to a problem.

Remember: While others often have worthwhile advice for you, ultimately you, your 99% self, your Smart Part, is the only one who knows which path is best for you.

> *". . . If you can trust yourself when all men doubt you,*
> *but make allowance for their doubting, too, then . . .*
> *you'll be a man, my son."*
> **(Rudyard Kipling, If)**

Assignment

Write the following on your 3x5 card. Focus on it several times a day.

- I am a perfect child of my creator doing my best to grow in this world of confused ego thinking.
- Nothing anyone says can change who I am
- Practice your movie scene explained under Do this: (see above)

MIRACLE TIP | WEEK ELEVEN
WHAT IS BELIEF?

"Nothing is easier than self-deceit.
For what each man wishes, that, he also believes to be true."
(Demosthenes, an ancient Greek statesman
from the fourth century)

A thought + same thought + same thought + same thought + same thought, which we continue to think over and over again = *Your beliefs.*

Your beliefs become YOUR truth, not THE Truth.

The problem is, most of the thoughts that became your beliefs were put there at a very young age, long before you had the ability to examine them for validity. Yet they run your life. People are constantly destroying relationships and even kill to support and maintain their unexamined beliefs which they think are the truth.

If your life is not working as you would like, you are generally functioning from false 1%, ego-based beliefs. Ninety-nine percent beliefs always bring peace and happiness.

Can you see, now, why it is silly to be hurt by unexamined beliefs of others and then use them to criticize yourself, just because you aren't living in accordance with their unexamined, unreliable belief system?

Assignment

Examine one of your beliefs, such as, "My religion and/or my philosophy is The Truth and those who believe otherwise are wrong." Consider what results it is bringing. Then consider the fact that Truth with a capitol "T" brings peace and freedom.

MIRACLE TIP | WEEK TWELVE
DANGER IN FALSE BELIEFS

"Human beings are perhaps never more frightening than when they are convinced beyond doubt that they are right."
(Laurens van der Post)

How can we know if our belief system is true? There is only one way to know . . . By the results it creates.

What results are we looking for? Freedom! You will be emotionally, mentally and spiritually free if your beliefs are **The Truth!** Your beliefs even effect your physical health. False beliefs can harm your health while True beliefs can help it.

"And ye shall know the truth
and the truth shall make you free"
(John 8:32).

All perception falls within the realm of illusion; truth comes by inspiration, or revelation, from the 99% world. With the vision of 20/20 hindsight, you may now realize you have been receiving some inspiration all along, but didn't recognize it as such.

If your beliefs result in making you unhappy, causing chaos and confusion, they come from the realm of illusion and are false. But being false does not mean they were wrong for they may have been the very wakeup call that helped you move forward.

When you begin to examine and replace dysfunctional beliefs, there can be some temporary discomfort. Why? Because your ego, your 1% thought system, is terrified of change and begins acting up making you feel you are doing something wrong.

This does not mean your new beliefs are false; it merely means that happiness may be delayed in showing up until the ego is quieted.

Assignment

Examine areas in your life that are causing you unhappiness. Be persistent in looking for the false belief behind them. Ask your higher self for help. It will help. Listen for the answer, which will come when you are in a calm state, or it may come through another person if spirit can't get through to you.

MIRACLE TIP | WEEK THIRTEEN
OUR MOST DAMAGING BELIEF

*"Thinking you are your body makes you a victim
of the world you see, and keeps you in fear."*
(Claudia T. Nelson-Evans)

What is your most damaging belief? It is the belief that you are your body. This belief is so damaging because . . .

1. It keeps you from looking for, and finding, the real you, which is so much more than the body.

2. Feeling limited depresses you because our deepest real self (our 99%) knows we are so much more . . . that we have unlimited potential.
3. It keeps you in fear.

- Fear you won't have all you need to care for this body . . . homes, food, clothes, etc.
- Fear your body is not good enough—that it's not the right size, shape, or color
- Fear of health problems and other harm that could come to the body
- Fear of aging and death

When living in fear, it is impossible to find out who you really are, for fear cuts you off from the source that reveals the path of understanding your True self, your 99% self.

If you don't find the real you, you will never find the true peace and happiness which we are striving for with these lessons. The Christian Bible tells us we are created in God's image and tells us God is Love. Ponder that for a while. It is deep and will come to make more sense as you work these lessons.

Assignment

Every day this week think of a funeral you have attended. Did you see the lifeless body in the casket? Ask yourself this:

- What is it that previously made that body move, think and grow?
- What happened to that thing that made that body think, act and grow?
- Which is most real; the cold lifeless body, or that life giving substance?

MIRACLE TIP | WEEK FOURTEEN
IF I AM NOT A BODY, WHO AM I?

"The opposite of seeing through the body's eyes is the vision of Christ, which reflects strength rather than weakness, unity rather than separation and love rather than fear."
(A Course in Miracles)

What is it that sees through different eyes and reflects strength, unity and lack of fear?

It is the real you, that is *not* the body. It is ***not*** your sad self!

You learned when you began these Miracle Tips that you are a two-part being, that the body is not the real you. ***You have a body, but you*** *are not your body! Your body is a tool, a learning device. The real you is sooo much more!*

The real you is the part that is missing from the body lying in a casket cold and lifeless. The lifeless body, when living, gave life to the ego, which kept that entity in fear and caused all of its confusion.

The missing part in a cold stiff body is our Smart Part, the 99% part, or, the Love-based self; the soul, the spirit, the real us. That is where we find our peace, power and purpose. I repeat, in your 99% thinking you see you are so much more—more grand, more expansive!

Only when thinking in the 1% thought system do you think you are a body. This concept may take some time to really digest and become useful. When it does, your thinking will dramatically change and you will feel so much freer.

Assignment

This week, give serious thought to what living in your 1% world has created. Give more serious thought to which part you want to rule your life . . . and why. What price are you willing to pay to find your Smart Part—the real you?

MIRACLE TIP | WEEK FIFTEEN
CONNECTING TO THE REAL YOU

"The ego world we see, and live in, is the world
of our Confused Part; it sees everything upside down
and backwards. It is this world that causes our pain.
Our Smart Part sees from a higher perspective."
(Claudia T. Nelson-Evans)

The Bible, the best-selling book ever written, tells us the only way to achieve freedom from the ego is to understand the pain and suffering it is causing.

Moving out of ego and connecting to our Smart Part takes time. Here are two steps to get started.

Step One: Recognize, really recognize, we are in a chaotic world that creates heart attacks, panic attacks, suicide and genocide. Getting this at a heart level provides motivation to see things differently.

Step Two: Develop the ability to answer the following question in the affirmative: "Am I willing to see things differently?"

This is one of our biggest challenges. The ego wants to keep us stuck in chaotic, "I'm right, you're wrong" thinking. Here ego remains in control. Overcoming our need to "be right" is not only a major step in connecting to our Smart Part; it is part of the price we pay for success.

Assignment

Test yourself this week. See how willing you are to see things differently. If another has a different point of view from yours, can you see any possible value in that perspective? Are you willing to alter your own perspective, or at least honor their perspective as having value?

UNDERSTANDING REACTIVE BEHAVIOR

"Everything can be taken from a man, or a woman but one thing: the last of human freedoms—to choose one's attitude in any given set of circumstances, to choose one's own way."
(Viktor Frankl)

Reactive behavior is impulsive and most often destructive, and generally brings negative consequences. It comes from our dark side, our 1% thinking. We know we have a dark side when we exhibit traits such as rage, jealousy, resentment, blaming and greed. **All negative behavior comes from our dark side and is fear-based.**

These reactive feelings arise in part from the denied parts of us which Carl Jung calls our shadow. *The Way of Mastery* and *A Course in Miracles* **both explain that reactive feelings come from a need for self-forgiveness.**

Reactive behavior begins to develop in childhood as we judge ourselves for negative feelings, then stuff the feelings to avoid the psychological pain our judgments produced. Stuffed feelings and self-judgment grow our ego. Our ego-based, lower self always lives in fear; fear of not having enough or being enough.

We encounter our ego, or shadow world, when we feel an unexplainable dislike for someone. These feelings give us a clue that buried feelings such as feeling not good enough or self-judgment are coming to the surface for healing . . . to free us.

These stuffed down feelings are like rocks in our shadow bag that weigh us down. I often refer to the bag as our Pandora's Box of furies.

Now the ego does something clever to make certain those unwanted feelings remain buried. It encourages us to blame and throw the rocks at the person who caused them to surface. Don't listen to your ego, fear-based 1% mind. Face the feelings honestly, heal them and be grateful for the one who helped them surface. This is how your freedom comes.

Ego is clever, it wants to keep us from looking inside and freeing ourselves of the negative feelings that keep us disempowered, allowing ego to remain in control. Ego wants job security.

Assignment

This week, simply notice when you are reacting and exhibiting any negative behaviors. Keep track of how many times you react negatively this week. Next week we will give a formula for overcoming reactive behavior.

MIRACLE TIP | WEEK SEVENTEEN

OVERCOMING REACTIVE BEHAVIOR

"Between stimulus and response there is a space.
In that space is our power to choose our responses.
In our responses are our growth and our freedom."
(Viktor Frankl)

The following very practical formula for overcoming reactive behavior comes from Kabbalistic teachings. It's a simple and user-friendly three-step process: **The STP Formula**

Step One: S . . . is for Stop. If you find yourself being reactive or negative this week, remember to stop. Count to 10 before reacting.

Step Two: T . . . is for Think. Think about the consequences of your behavior. Later think about what is unhealed in you, like your own self-judgmental issues that could be causing you to project your negative feelings onto others in reactive behavior.

Step Three: P . . . is for **pro**-act. Replace negative reactive thinking and behavior with something positive. Say a kind word, do a kind deed, simply smile. Or, just zipper your lips, if that is the best you can do at the moment.

Remember: A moment of patience can ward off great disaster while a moment of impatience can ruin a whole life.

Assignment

Recall a time when you reacted negatively in a tense situation. Remember the consequences of your reactive behavior. Did it work out well? Remember this formula, put it on your card, work with it and watch it change your life.

MIRACLE TIP | WEEK EIGHTEEN

HONORING DIFFERENCES

"[An] underdeveloped country is not inappropriate
in any way [nor are what we consider undeveloped people].
If [they] have different desires and different standards,
[they] are not lesser than—just different. We did not all
come to do it the same way. We did not all come to be
alike. We came as a diverse bunch of Non-Physical Energies
wanting different experiences [for our personal growth]."
(Abraham Hicks)

All too often we think our perspective is *the truth*, but it is only our truth. All we really have is our perspective based on our programming and our experiences and how we choose, or have been taught, to interpret them.

It is easy to see why people have different points of view, as they have chosen different experiences and have had different programming. While their perspectives may not work for you, they work for them until they don't—so how can anyone judge them as wrong?

Understanding this makes it easy to accept and honor different perspectives. It also gives us an opportunity to learn from each other. If each party puts their perspective on the table, each honoring the other's perspective, perhaps after considering all perspectives they can come closer to *the truth* than they could with only their own point of view or perspective. Coming to Truth is one value of diverse perspectives.

Assignment

Examine one perspective (belief) that is not working for you in a relationship, such as believing that in a good relationship both parties need to think alike. Find at least one new way of looking at a relationship from a different perspective using the methods you have learned so far.

MIRACLE TIP | WEEK NINETEEN
BEHAVIOR IS A CHOICE

"Behavior is a choice; it isn't who you are."
(*The Way of Mastery*)

There is a popular story about an old Cherokee man who is teaching his grandson about life:

"A fight is going on inside me," the grandfather said to the boy.

He continued, "It is a terrible fight and it is between two wolves. One is evil—he is anger, envy, sorrow, regret, greed, arrogance, self-pity, guilt, resentment, inferiority, lies, false pride, superiority, and **ego.**"

He continued further, "The other is good—he is joy, peace, love, hope, serenity, humility, kindness, benevolence, empathy, generosity, truth, compassion, and faith.

The same fight is going on inside you—and inside every other person, too."

The grandson thought about it for a minute and then asked his grandfather: "Which wolf will win?" The old Cherokee simply replied, **"The one you feed."**

Perhaps negative behavior is learned and comes from parroting behavior learned by observing those in authority. Being authority figures, you believed their beliefs and actions were those to emulate. Perhaps behavior comes from your own repressed, denied feelings. Whatever the case, when you see your beliefs, or behaviors, are not creating the results you desire, you can always choose to believe and behave differently.

Choice is one thing no one can ever take away from you. It is your one true freedom. You can choose to think with our 1% ego, fear-based mind, or you can choose to think and act with our 99% mind. Consider the result of each way of thinking.

Assignment

Observe every one of your decisions today. Before making any decision ask yourself . . . which wolf do I want to influence my decision? Choose.

MIRACLE TIP | WEEK TWENTY
CHALLENGING OUR BELIEFS

"When your life begins to disintegrate, ego yells, "You're having a breakdown." Spirit answers, "No, you are having a breakthrough, for ego is dying as you begin challenging old beliefs."
(Claudia T. Nelson Evans)

When your life seems to disintegrate, it is a good thing. It simply lets you know that you, like the tree, are dropping the old to create nourishment for new growth. It is only at such times, propelled by your discomfort, that you step out of old ruts and start searching for different or better ways or Truer answers and new growth.

As always, when this happens ego frowns, steps in, distorts the truth, cries "no, no, don't do this" and puts you in fear. As always, ego is confused and, as always, wants job security; that of being in control of your life.

While ego is frowning, your Smart Part is smiling. It knows the old responses in you, triggered by loss, must die to support new growth, Nature teaches us how to respond to loss.

> When a tree loses its leaves, the tree doesn't scream, "No, no, why do I have to go through this every year?" It allows them to gently fall, knowing the leaves will turn to compost creating the fertilizer for it to grow bigger and more beautiful the next year. A lesson from the trees. As our old lives die, the dead disintegrates and creates new growth.

Assignment

Sit and meditate on the trees and ask the spirit inside to always remember the lessons of the trees. Draw a smiling tree on your card with falling leaves. Ponder how something you have lost has caused new positive growth in you. (If you are unaccustomed to meditating and do not have a favorite practice, go to the Appendix where I have given you a very effective meditative practice.)

MIRACLE TIP | WEEK TWENTY-ONE
GREAT THINKERS ON BELIEF

"Convictions are more dangerous enemies of truth than lies."
(Fredrich Wilhelm Nietzsche)

"Nothing is easier than self-deceit. For what each man wishes, that he also believes to be true." (Demosthenes)

"A belief is only a thought you think over and over again until it becomes a belief." (*The Way of Mastery*)

"There are two ways to slide easily through life: to believe everything or to doubt everything; both ways save us from thinking." (Alfred Korzybski)

"This is how humans are: we question our beliefs, except for the ones we really believe, and those we never think to question." (Orson Scott Card)

"Men never do evil so thoroughly as when they do it for conscience sake."(Blaise Pascal Pensées, 1670)

"He does not believe who does not according to his belief." (Thomas Fuller)

Assignment
Ponder these quotes. Apply one of them to your life.

MIRACLE TIP | WEEK TWENTY-TWO
ALL ABOUT SIN

"Sin is one of the most used and least understood
words in our vocabulary."
(Claudia T. Nelson-Evans)

What can we say about sin? We could talk about how to do it, why we shouldn't, how much fun it is, or how much pain it causes. Of course, we've heard sermons on some of the above and developed rationalizations for the rest. What really needs to be talked about is how little we understand it.

Sin is an archery term. It simply means if the archer has missed the mark, he has sinned. For you, it means that your mis-thinking has caused you to miss the mark, or target, of where you wanted to be. This simply means that you, like the archer, need to practice to get it right.

Ego plays another trick on you with the word "sin." Ego uses the word sin to put you into fear . . . fear that you are not okay. Ego turns sin into guilt, shame and eventually depression. These are all attributes of fear. Fear separates you from yourself, each other and your creator . . . again keeping you disempowered, leaving ego in control, and you disconnected from your higher power who gives you the help you need to get things 'right' and hit the bulls eye.

"No experience you have ever had has proven your
unworthiness to be supported, to be loved, by your creator."
(The Way of Mastery)

By taking the word sin out of context from the whole of Christianity, it does more harm than good—until you begin to add the word repentance to the mix. Then one must understand what the word "repent" means.

Repent means to think again. Yes, think again! For thinking changes your feelings, feelings change your action and action changes your results. Repentance isn't a punishment for what many call "sin"; it is a gift for healing "sin."

So if you have missed the mark, and your arrows landed where you didn't want them to land, rethink where you went wrong and keep practicing until you get it right.

Assignment

Consider all the damage the ego has created with its misinterpretation of sin—not only for you, but your loved ones. Correct your thinking and be the example for others to follow.

MIRACLE TIP | WEEK TWENTY-THREE

NEVER ALLOW ANOTHER PERSON TO DEFINE YOU

"Many of the faults you see in another, dear readers,
are your own nature reflected in them."
(Rumi)

Why do you allow another to define you? Could it be because you have been taught from birth to be obedient, to do what your parents, your teachers and your preachers tell you to do? You are taught how to think about nearly everything.

Have you accepted this dictate and allowed others to tell you how to think about yourself? Or, if they are criticizing you, are they only bringing to the surface your own hidden self-judgments which they are projecting onto you? Whatever the case, don't allow it.

You may want to consider what they have said for any smidgen of truth it contains. If you detect any truth in their opinion, don't deny it, don't judge it; correct it, then delete their opinion. Then ask your higher self to help you see who you really are.

You are not your flaws!

Your higher self will tell you that the *real* you is a perfect child of God, totally innocent, loved and loveable, powerful and unlimited.

The reason another's opinion is generally so inaccurate is because it is a projection of how they view themselves, and tells you more about them than it does about you. Psychologists would call these overused defense mechanisms denial and projection. These are psychological defense mechanisms used to deny that they have a problem and instead project it onto someone else. However, their often-negative opinions do have purpose. They push you to find out who you really are.

Assignment

Another week of self-examination. How have you allowed others to define you? Ask your higher self to reveal the Truth to you. When you ask yourself questions, your Higher Self responds well. It will answer in its own time and its own way. Don't try to force it, just stay observant and in touch with the 99%. Meditation helps with this process. (See Appendix.)

MIRACLE TIP | WEEK TWENTY-FOUR
A NEW VIEW OF LOVE

"Stop wasting energy trying to love God. That will not do it for you. Stop wasting energy trying to learn how to love another. That will not do it for you. And . . . please refrain from all attempts to get anyone to believe you love them!"
(The Way of Mastery)

Love is something we all want more of but few, if any of us, fully understand.

- Einstein believed Love was the United Field (that from which all things are created).
- Jerry Jampolsky, M.D., a psychiatrist says, "Love is Letting Go of Fear."
- *The Way of Mastery* explains love in a most sensible and useful manner, which challenges most traditional concepts, but removes the strain of trying to get or give love.

Our 1% concept of love is upside down and backwards, as is every-thing in our 1% world. This 99% concept of love is lasting and perma-nent, unlike any concept or everything else in our 1% world, which is always temporary and can be here today and gone tomorrow.

Love isn't something we get through our striving; it is something we find deep within ourselves. It is who we are. To be love begins with a decision.

When you find love within, "learn to nurture that self which speaks of joy and truth so that your words and your actions and your very pres-ence always uplift another, so that when another walks into the room in which you are sitting, standing or moving they feel like a breath of fresh air just hit them, even if you have not lifted a finger… Then you are auto-matically giving love and will automatically receive it back, no striving involved. Love cannot be contained, only allowed. Love allows all things, trusts all things, embraces all things and therefore transcends all things." (*The Way of Mastery*)

It is by removing the fears blocking the love, allowing the love that you are to shine forth, that creates its magic effortlessly. The effort is in loving ourselves and nurturing our loving part; then the ability to truly love others follows naturally without effort.

We must eliminate our fears. Fear and love cannot live in the same person at the same time any more than two objects can occupy the same space at the same time.

Assignment

Write the quotes on a 3x5 card. Read them every morning upon waking and ponder them during the day. Do the same in the evening. Practice them the best you can. You will get better and better at it with practice and it will get easier and easier.

MIRACLE TIP | WEEK TWENTY-FIVE
FINDING YOUR DESTINY

"So that is what destiny is: Simply the fulfillment of the potentialities of the energies of our system."
(Joseph Campbell)

Many want to fulfill their destiny and struggle for years to try to find what and where it is. Joseph Campbell nails it with his quote. It is simply finding our true selves. There, in your loving self, is hidden your destiny, your potential *and* your specific talents needed for your particular mission on planet earth, should you choose to accept it.

Too often, we put the cart before the horse and try to find our destiny in the 1% world where it can never be found. It is like trying to find shampoo in the toilet. One must connect to the 99% self where all truth is found.

Everyone's mutual destiny is to reconnect to whom they really are. And we each have a "mission" unique to us. Ask your higher power to reveal what your specific mission, destiny or purpose is on planet earth.

This is the Hero's Journey that Joseph Campbell writes about, taught using myths as analogy.

Each lesson is designed to get you closer and closer to your 99% world. You will know if you are there by how you feel. You will feel positive emotions and feel at peace. If you are in the 1% your emotions will be negative. Your feelings are your barometer to tell you where you are.

You will go in and out of the 99% and learn to stay there longer and longer. In this world of form it is almost impossible to live there all the time as our bodies have to survive on planet earth. When we have completed the 99% journey and are there 100% of the time, we will no longer need the body. It is simply a tool for learning and growing through our experiences.

This is an experiential journey *One-Minute Miracles* is providing for you. Keep up the good work. Yes, it is work, nothing worthwhile comes without effort. In our instant gratification society, you might wish to forget that. If you do, you may never find your destiny. Just as the concert pianist achieves mastery by practicing the piano daily, you achieve mastery over yourself by practicing your assignments daily. The prize is worth the price.

Assignment

Take the week off and congratulate yourself for coming this far. It is not being prideful; it is being respectful of yourself.

MIRACLE TIP | WEEK TWENTY-SIX

BECOMING MASTER OVER OURSELVES

"We fail to realize mastery is not about perfection. It is about a process, a journey. The master is one who stays on the path day after day, year after year. The master is one who is willing to try and fail and try again for as long as he or she lives."
(George Leonard)

George Leonard's quote reminds me or one of my favorite poems: **RISKS**

> To laugh is to risk appearing a fool
> To weep is to risk appearing sentimental
> To reach out to another is to risk involvement
> To expose feelings is to risk exposing your true self

To place your ideas, your dreams before a crowd is to risk
their loss
To love is to risk not being loved in return
To live is to risk dying
To hope is to risk despair
To try is to risk failure

But risks must be taken because the greatest hazard in life is to risk nothing. The person who risks nothing, does nothing, has nothing and is nothing, when viewed with 1% thinking. They might avoid suffering and sorrow but they cannot learn, change, grow, love and live. Chained by their certitudes they are a slave; they have forfeited their freedom.

Assignment

If you have gotten this far in the book, you have already taken a risk. Congratulations. Take another risk this week, perhaps one suggested in the RISKS poem. Line four is a good one.

THE MEANING OF RESPONSIBILITY

"Look at the word 'response ability' the ability
to choose your response. Highly proactive people recognize
that responsibility. They do not blame circumstances,
conditions or conditioning for their behavior."
(Steven Covey)

Do you understand what the ability to choose your responses really means? It means you have the ability to respond to any situation with love or fear. Those are your only two choices as any negative reaction is always fear-based. Which you choose determines the life you create. Your thoughts are the seeds from which your life grows. Nothing is impossible when you plant 99% thought seeds. Love thoughts produce a good life, Fear thoughts produce the opposite. Nature exemplifies this principle.

> If you plant unhealthy vegetable seeds, you get unhealthy vegetables. If you plant unhealthy thoughts you get an unhealthy life. Negative thought seeds like criticism, judgment, fear and blame are unhealthy thought seeds. You are responsible for the seeds you plant and the results you get.

Positive thought seeds like understanding, forgiveness, compassion and love are healthy thought seeds which produce healthy lives.

"Mind control is the result of self-discipline and habit. You either control your mind or it controls you. There is no halfway compromise."
(Napoleon Hill)

Helps for thought-control: When you feel a negative fear thought surfacing:

1. Sing a song. Have a special one ready that lifts your spirits.
2. Recite a special uplifting poem. Have one ready.
3. Continue to say Love, Love, Love over and over until your negative thoughts are under control.
4. Think of a wonderful, happy time you have experienced.
5. Pray/meditate; ask your higher self what is coming up for healing

6. OR, don't react to; or judge your thoughts. Simply ask your higher self to help you explore them to find their fear-based origin, then, reprogram yourself with the methods you are learning. This is the healthiest option, but may need to be a second step at a later time.

I will continue to remind you . . . Thoughts—>Feelings—>Actions—>Results. Translated this means: Your Thoughts create your feelings. Feelings create your actions, or reactions. Actions or reactions, create the results you are experiencing in your life.

"If you are not wholly joyous, it could be because
you have elected to use the power of your mind
to think differently than your creator."
(The Way of Transformation)

Assignment

Monitor your thoughts all day. Watch to see what they are creating

MIRACLE TIP | WEEK TWENTY–EIGHT
AWAKEN TO WHOM YOU ARE

"The pathway of awakening, no matter the form it takes,
is always a retraining of the mind."
(The Way of Transformation)

You are sooooo much more than you think; you are smarter, stronger and braver than you believe you are. Why don't you understand this? Maybe you are just lazy or tired. But, I doubt it, or you wouldn't be reading this book. ☺

It is because of your **mis**-programming? Partially. But let us take it a step deeper. We can't blame anyone. You have always had agency to choose how to perceive things. And others have had the agency to choose how they present things to you. The problem is . . .

Those doing the programming have presented things in such an enticing manner that you have chosen to adopt their perceptions and hold onto them until you find . . . they are not working well, causing only pain and fear.

For example: Through enticing programming we have chosen to believe that having money, the perfect body, the best clothes, etc., will buy happiness. You spend your life chasing these things but see others still have more, or look better, causing you to continually fear you are not good enough.

Thank Edward Bernays, the father of advertising and propaganda for much of this thinking. He was taught by his uncle, Dr. Sigmund Freud, how to manipulate the public's mind into purchasing their goods or services. Bernays came to America to teach businesses how to manipulate the mind to sell their goods. We bought into the manipulations—until now. Experience has taught us, through opposition, that buying things has not created happiness.

As you are reprogramming your mind, I remind you again to study the thought wheel and think deeply about its implications as you are **undoing** your mis-programming. So through our experiences, we begin to wake up. Seeing clearly, we look for a better way of thinking and being, and here we are. It is all good.

Assignment

For an overview of Edward Bernays's work, go to:

1. YouTube: Search for the *Century of Self* documentary by Adam Curtis
2. Amazon also has the documentary
3. Wikipedia also has the information (search for "Century of Self.")

MIRACLE TIP | WEEK TWENTY-NINE
PERSONAL GROWTH AND MONEY

*"Every time you blame, justify or complain
you are slitting your financial throat."*
(Robert Kiyosaki, *Rich Dad, Poor Dad*)

If negative thinking and behavior, a byproduct of fear, hinders your ability to make money, eliminating them helps your pocket book. Any self-improvement veteran knows that taking responsibility and eliminating blaming, judging, justifying and being the victim is foundational to personal achievement.

How do these above-named vices slit our financial throat?

If we are indulging in the above negatives, it is a sign we are living in fear. All negative behavior is fear-based. Fear sets off negative vibrations which connect with other negative fear vibrations, which increases fear. Results produced through fear seldom bring satisfying results.

To attempt to make satisfying healthy money before you have done your personal growth work is putting the cart before the horse. You create the good and lasting with 99% thinking.

Those who make money with a 1%, victim mentality are generally fearful of losing it so it is rarely satisfying, becomes an addiction to more, and enough is never enough.

How do we overcome our fears? Ralph Waldo Emerson had a solution. He said: **"Do what you are afraid to do and the death of fear is certain."**

That does not mean, however, that you take a stupid risk. Fear can be a warning not to go too close to the edge of a cliff. Emerson was speaking of facing our unfounded psychological fears.

Doing this inner personal work, confronting ourselves and our fears, takes courage. Therefore, continuing our personal growth, will help the pocket book. If you find that it is difficult to get something done, essential to your success, it is most always because of an unidentified fear.

Assignment

This week notice any resistance you have to making positive change, or progress in your job, your family, or towards a goal. Ask your higher power to help you identify and overcome the fear causing the resistance. "Ask and ye *shall* receive" (John 16:24).

MIRACLE TIP | WEEK THIRTY
A NEW VIEW ON MONEY

"Money is a good servant but a bad master."
(Gretchen Rubin)

Have you ever lost all your money and feared you could never survive without it, believing your security was in your money? If so, you have likely learned, as I did, that money is not where your security is. It can be here today and gone tomorrow.

But you have, or will eventually learn, your security is not in anything that can be here today and gone tomorrow.

So where is your security? You must have food, clothes and shelter to survive on planet earth, all the things money buys. When you step out of your fears, out of the 1% thinking you connect to real power to create whatever you need through 99% thinking. There, you can recreate what you need.

In his book, *Overachievement,* Dr. John Eliot gives explains that high performance people, who have stepped out of their fears, do the following:

- Eat stress like a power bar
- Turn off the cerebral cortex so ego can't use that part of the brain to cause them to go into fear and doubt themselves
- Focus on their task, forget everything else and trust themselves

The magic word is trust; it's the opposite of fear. Personal transformation work requires that we find and face our fears. Once found, we can eliminate them. Eliminating them creates a vacuum for trust to enter. Personal transformational work can help the pocketbook and so much more.

When you have transformed through your personal growth work you will be living in your 99% world much of the time. When you are in the 99%, tapped in and turned on, what you need will show up effortlessly and often mysteriously, with or without money. And you will be a happy giver.

Giving and receiving are the same. The more you have the more you can give. **Give what you have to give, whether it be time, talent or money, etc., and you will get what you need.**

Always Remember: "A Wise man should have money in his head, not in his heart." (Jonathan Swift), and "Through money and power you can't solve all problems. Problems must be solved with the human [mind] and heart." (Dali Lama)

Assignment

Be honest with yourself with no self-judgment and decide if you own your money or if your money owns you.

MIRACLE TIP | WEEK THIRTY-ONE
THE POWER OF CHOICE

"There is choice you have to make in everything
you do. So keep in mind that in the end,
the choice you make, makes you."
(John Wooden)

You don't always have control over your situation. But you always have a choice of how you view it and how you will respond to it.

Do you see yourself as a victim if your past experiences have been challenging and unpleasant?

Do you fear the future?

Can you only be happy if you are in moments of genius?

Each moment can change us, but we can choose how it changes us.

Your past is gone. The future never comes; it only shows up as the present.

Make new decisions in the present, the now.

Four Steps of Moving from Victim to Victor:

1. **Choose:** Am I going to be victorious over my situation, or a victim of it?
2. **Grieve** but don't blame and don't stay stuck in your grief.
3. **Focus** on solutions and never the problem.
4. **Practice** and refine your solutions until the problem is solved.

Ultimately, we are working towards mastering our thoughts so we no longer have negative feelings which cause negative actions which cause negative results.

Assignment

Put these four steps on your card: Meditate on the four steps. Practice them and use them on all challenges you are facing.

MIRACLE TIP | WEEK THIRTY-TWO

RECOGNIZING FEARS
THAT HOLD US BACK

"If you are depressed you live in the past,
if you feel anxious, you live in the future.
If you feel peaceful, you live in the now."
(Lao-Tzu)

A Course in Miracles teaches that there are only two emotions, love and fear. Kabbalistic mystical teachings teach the same. Therefore, any time a negative emotion arises, if we reduce it to its lowest common denominator, we have fear.

Guilt is one manifestation of fear—fear we did something wrong and are, therefore, not good enough. Fear of the future is another indication we don't feel good enough to create a future we desire.

Start here if negative emotions arise. Ask:

- What am I afraid of?
- Am I afraid I am not good enough?
- Am I afraid I won't have enough?

Know your higher self will help you to see what fear is coming up for healing. "Ask and Ye shall receive." Ask where the fear came from and for courage to face and overcome it.

Close relationships often bring up our fears in the form of conflict. View these as a gift. We can't fix what we can't see. Be grateful. Don't make the one bringing up your fears wrong. Thank them.

> *"Relationships help expose our guilt and fears that squeeze the life out of us; relationships are a blessing."*
> **(Claudia Nelson-Evans)**

Assignment

Do the work of asking the questions under **start here** every day. Wait and watch for the answers to come. Don't try to force them. They will generally come when you are in a relaxed more peaceful state of mind. When they do, the antidote to healing is most often to see them with more mature eyes and change your thinking about them. Listen well! The answer will *never* be to try to change the other person.

MIRACLE TIP | WEEK THIRTY-THREE

WHERE WE FIND PEACE AND HAPPINESS

*"Perfect peace can come only from the soul's desire
to acknowledge the decision to value the Truth
and live it. Nothing else can bring the soul
to the completion of its peace."*
(*The Way of Transformation*)

It is your ego-based fear thought system trying to make you think it is what you own, wear, consume, where you can travel, or the "perfect" relationship, that brings peace and happiness. It sometimes makes us think happiness comes from pleasing everyone—or living a life that someone else desires for you. That is 1% thinking. Ninety-nine-percent thinking is where Truth with a capitol T is found; the Truth that brings genuine peace and happiness.

When we live in our ego thought system we wear ourselves out looking for happiness where it cannot be found. It is like looking in the dishwasher for milk. You just can't find it there no matter how hard you try—unless you have Alzheimer's, then I doubt you would be reading this.

Again, the ego-based fear thought system has only 1% of truth and knows very little about true happiness. Also remember that anything in this world of form, meaning anything you can see with your physical eyes, can be here today and gone tomorrow. While some things can bring a moment of pleasure, everything in our 1% world of form is temporary. That means everything, including you.

Authentic peace and happiness comes from connecting to your 99% thought system, which contains 99% of truth and all positive attitudes like love, peace, grace and gratitude. The 99% you knows that bodily pleasures are temporary at best and never bring authentic happiness, because you are not your body. (Review Miracle Tip Fourteen)

What we all really want is authentic love. That is what brings authentic peace and happiness. Ego tries to convince us that having all the worldly stuff will make us more lovable. In Truth, others will authentically love you when you first authentically love them.

Love is the ultimate Truth. To love others you must first connect to whom you are, and learn to love yourself. Only then can you give authentic love to others. Then you will get it back. Remember giving and receiving are the same thing. Trying to do it any other way is putting the cart before the horse. You must first love yourself because you can't give what you don't have.

"Happiness cannot be traveled to, owned, worn
or consumed. Happiness is the spiritual experience
of living every minute with love, grace and gratitude."
(Denis Waitley)

Assignment

Choose one loving attribute found in the 99% world of thought and focus on it all week. For example, you could choose to see the good in someone you have judged negatively. *If you can't do it, ask yourself this question; Have I learned to love myself sufficiently?*

MIRACLE TIP | WEEK THIRTY-FOUR
PEACE AND FORGIVENESS

"To forgive is to release another from the perceptions
you have been projecting upon them. It is therefore,
an act of forgiving one's self of ones projections."
(*The Way of Mastery*)

In *The Way of Mastery* it further states that:

". . . forgiveness is an essential key to healing. The opposite of for-giveness is judgment, and judgment always creates separation and guilt. Judgment will evoke a sense of guilt in the one who is doing the judging as well as the one being judged, unless they are perfectly awake.

Each time you judge anything or anyone, you have literally elicited guilt within *yourself.* Because there is a place within you, yet still, that knows the perfect purity, of your brother and sister, and sees quite clearly that *all things within the human realm are either the extension of love or a cry for help and healing.*

When you judge you have moved out of alignment with what is true. And you have already declared that this [judgment] is true about yourself. Therefore, to practice forgiveness actually cultivates the quality of consciousness in which you finally come to forgive yourself.

> *"Beloved friend, these things are of critical importance.*
> *For anyone who enters into a so-called 'spiritual path' must*
> *eventually face and deal with their deep need for forgiveness.*
> *For there is no one who walks the earth who has not been*
> *touched by the poison of judgment." (The Way of Mastery)*

Hopefully, you now see the connection between happiness and forgiveness. True forgiveness allows you to begin to love yourself. When you love yourself, you have love to give and will then get love in return. There is no happiness without love. Forgiving is essential to loving and loving is essential for happiness. Remember: *To understand everything is to forgive everything.* (Buddha)

Assignment

Think of one person you have need to forgive. Spend time meditating about this person and asking for help in knowing how to truly forgive him/her. It may or may not be wise to talk to them in person, but they will get it intuitively if you don't do it in person. Keep working on it until you feel it is sincere and complete. Then notice how you feel. (See Appendix for a suggested meditation).

MIRACLE TIP | WEEK THIRTY-FIVE
LOVE IS OUR DEEPEST DESIRE

*"When you love people and have the desire to make
a profound, positive impact upon the world,
then you will have accomplished the meaning to life."*
(Sasha Azevedo)

Finding your true desires is not easy. Why? They have been programmed out of you. You now hopefully understand that wants and desires are not the same. I will remind you that: *Wants generally come from 1% thinking and are often selfish and may ultimately cause you pain. Desires are essential for creating in the 99% world and should be **encouraged!***

"Prayer is the soul's sincere desire,
  Uttered or unexpressed,
  Emotion of a hidden fire,
  That trembles in our breast."[1]

There is one healthy, essential universal 99% desire everyone possesses, although many have repressed that need to love and be loved, because of past hurts. To be loved, you must give love away. The more you give love, the more you get for yourself. It is a universal law. Getting and giving are the same. (See the Road to Iosepa in Section 3)

The more love you have, the more you have to give away. All other desires then fall into their rightful place when you are connected to the 99% world of love. All knowledge is found in this 99% world, including your other true desires.

Again, I remind you, these lessons are designed to assist you in getting to this place of love where you understand and create your deepest desires. Only here can you find the true foundation of all genuine success and happiness. But, never underestimate the value of experiences in the 1% world, no matter how difficult or painful. They create the experiences that help you get to where you want to be. All experience is good!

Assignment

Pray and/or meditate daily on the subject of genuine love and ask for help in achieving it. Practice being loving. In all your interactions this week, especially when you don't feel like it. (See Appendix for suggested meditation.)

---

1   "Prayer is the Soul's Sincere Desire," though written in 1818 by James Montgomery, was officially published in a hymnal entitled The Christian Psalmist, published in 1825. However, it should be noted the hymn also showed up in hymns sung in Sunday school as well as in the 1819 edition of Treatise on Prayer.

MIRACLE TIP | WEEK THIRTY-SIX

SEE YOURSELF AS A LOVING PERSON

"The greatest gift you can give another is the gift
of unconditional love and acceptance."
(Brian Tracy)

While you are learning to genuinely love, you can fake it until you make it. But it is not really faking it because you are practicing what you want to become, which you truly already are; you are just learning to connect with that love.

It takes time to feel that love at a deep emotional level, especially love for yourself. But if you begin to picture yourself as a loving person, and do loving things, you will become genuinely loving.

Another reminder: You can't truly love another until you love yourself. You can't give what you don't have to give. The beauty and mystery is when you give love to others, you give love to yourself. Giving and getting are one.

> *Thus, you learn to love yourself by giving love to others and the more you love yourself, the more you can give it to others and the more you can love yourself.*

Be patient with yourself and keep growing, which you are doing by practicing these weekly One-Minute Miracles. **"Love grows as we grow."** (Claudia T. Nelson-Evans)

Assignment

Each time you feel like reacting to a potentially negative situation. Stop, Think, and Pro-act. (Miracle Tip Seventeen). Figure out a way to respond lovingly before you speak.

MIRACLE TIP | WEEK THIRTY–SEVEN

CREATING DESIRES FROM YOUR 99% WORLD

"To connect to your Smart Part, your 99% world
of thought, you must remove the obstacles
that keep you disconnected . . . your FEARS."
(Claudia T. Nelson-Evans)

The light world (the 99% world) we are trying to reach has a thick veil we must penetrate. There are ways to poke holes in that veil and let light shine through until we have enough light to completely remove it and create our desires.

Question: How does one poke holes in this veil to let the light through?

Answer: Keep allowing your fears to emerge; keep facing them and altering the thinking and behavior patterns that created the fears. It is those fears that keep the veil solid and in place. This veil is created and maintained by our fears. The veil is our fears.

Question: How does one eliminate the dysfunctional thinking, creating the fears standing between you and the light?

Answer: By Transforming thinking patterns. The previous tips, as well as the remaining miracle tips, will assist you in removing yourself from your 1% world of dysfunctional thinking by showing you how to access your 99% world of thinking.

Another benefit of this 99% higher world of thought is that you won't feel victimized by the tumultuous changes we are all experiencing in our world today. You will understand that is simply the old dysfunctional world dying to make way for a wonderful new peaceful and prosperous world.

Assignment

Monitor your feelings this week. Your feelings are your barometer to inform you which thought system you are living in. Negative feelings tell you that you are connected to the 1% world. Ask: What fear is behind these thoughts and feelings? Then reprogram.

MIRACLE TIP | WEEK THIRTY-EIGHT
CONNECTING TO THE WORLD OF LIGHT AND LOVE

"Never forget that the Holy Spirit does not depend
on your words. He understands the requests
of your heart, and answers them."
(A Course in Miracles)

A Course in Miracles, Kabbalistic teachings and *The Way of Mastery all*
teach **there are only two emotions, Love and Fear.** Therefore, any time
a negative emotion arises, if you reduce it to its lowest common denominator, you have fear.

If a negative emotion arises, know the spirit inside of you will help
you see what fear behind the emotion is coming up for healing. "Ask and
ye shall receive." *But, ask with a sincere heart.* You may not receive your

answer immediately; it will come when you are in the right state of mind and are ready to understand and accept the answer. Or, as noted earlier, the answer may come through another person.

Fear and love are unlike energies. Only like energies connect. Therefore, to connect to the 99% world of light, to receive answers from your 99% world you must be on the same energy wave length, which is love. Meditation helps you suspend fears and connect to a love vibration.

When a negative emotion comes up, start your analysis by asking:

- **What am I really afraid of?**
- **Am I afraid I am not good enough?**
- **Am I afraid I won't have enough?**

Remember, close relationships often bring up your fears in the form of conflict. These repressed feelings are repressed emotions, emotional rocks in your Pandora's bag surfacing for healing. Often, when your rocks come up, you want to throw them at the person who is bringing them to the surface. Don't. They are giving you a gift by bringing up your fear rocks to free you. Be grateful. It's your ego wanting to throw the rocks. Your higher self wants to dissolve them.

Assignment

Do the work of asking the questions above in bold print. in paragraph four. Wait for the answer and go to work healing the fear. Realize your fear isn't real and change how you look at it.

MIRACLE TIP | WEEK THIRTY-NINE
AN ATTITUDE OF GRATITUDE

*"Gratitude turns what we have into enough, and more.
It turns denial into acceptance, chaos into order, confusion
into clarity. It makes sense of our past, brings peace
for today, and creates a vision for tomorrow."*
(Melody Beattie)

Humanity wears itself out chasing after more of something. More money, more sex, more power, more stuff, more prestige and/or more of what they think is love. Why? Because . . .

. . . they are trying to fill a black hole inside by filling it with something on the outside; a black hole created because they have become disconnected from their real selves. Only reconnecting to this real self will heal them and bring them what they really want, genuine love, peace and happiness. Looking for it in the 1% world of form is like looking for a fish swimming in a tree.

It is most likely clear to you by now, that you can never find what you were looking for in your 1% fear-based world of form. It is also most likely clear by now that your search for your missing 99% self would never have begun if life had been too easy, and you would still be like the rest of humanity spending your precious time chasing more.

> *One of the most common and most overlooked addictions*
> *in our world is the addiction to MORE.*

Gratitude is a great start in healing the black hole inside and overcoming the addiction to more. Refrain from focusing on what you don't have. Give gratitude every day for what you do have, a comfortable home, food, a family, friends, clothing, a good book, knowledge that is coming forth, and the trials that brought you to this point, etc.

Buddha reminds us, " Enough is a feast." Be especially grateful for your difficult circumstances and those spurring you on to find a higher way of living.

> *"He is a wise man who does not grieve for the things*
> *which he has not, but rejoices for those which he has."*
> **(EPICETUS)**

Assignment

Make a list of all the things you have to be grateful for. Add something to this list each day this week. Think on it often.

MIRACLE TIP | WEEK FORTY

WHAT MOTIVATES US TO SEEK THE LIGHT

"Desire is the key to motivation . . . but,
it's determination and commitment to an unrelenting
pursuit of your goal—a commitment to excellence—
that will enable you to attain the success you seek."
(Mario Andretti)

It was the trauma of the tiger chasing the man who is ready to take a hunk out of his butt that motivated the man to run his hardest. Without that threat would the man have been motivated to expend the energy to run his hardest? Not likely.

It is only when we are threatened when the things in our previously comfortable 1% world of form begin to break down that we are we motivated to find a safer place to dwell; a place where tigers don't try to take a bite of you.

We know, in this world of form, anything can be here today and gone tomorrow, including our butts. This kind of threat of loss often provides the motivation to put in the effort to find our 99% world, the place where we not only find safety, but become emotionally and mentally healthy. We are all a bit insane while living in the 1% ego world of fear and confusion.

The famous Psychiatrist, Dr. Carl Jung, called this psychological/spiritual growth process of becoming mentally, emotionally and spiritually healthy, the INDIVIDUATION PROCESS.

Note to Reader: Jung saw individuation as a two-step process. Many, have experienced the Individuation Process as a three-step process. An additional step came to me through my experience and practice of Jung's active imagination art, the art from which he gained much of his knowledge.

The tigers in our lives provide the motivation to begin understanding and using Jung's three stage Individuation Process to become safe and healthy. The three stages are:

1. Disintegration
2. Segregation (the one I received through my Active Imagination Art)
3. Reintegration

We will discuss these three phases in the next three lessons and how each is necessary to transform your life and catapult you out of the 1% world.

Assignment

In your personal preparation time, recall an experience in your life, a loss, or trauma of any kind, and look for the positive benefit you received. There is always a blessing that comes from trauma and heartache if you look for it. This book was born from learning how to find blessings in and overcoming my own traumas.

MIRACLE TIP | WEEK FORTY-ONE
THE DISINTREGRATION PROCESS

*"Everything in this world of form is unstable,
leaving us fearful and insecure. This gives us a burning
desire to find something better, motivating us
to find something permanent that we can trust."*
(Claudia T. Nelson-Evans)

Here we will discuss the first stage of Dr. Jung's Individuation Process that catapults us into a better world, one we can trust, the one where we become emotionally and spiritually healthy. It is a necessary process enabling us to become a frequent visitor of this 99% world.

We will visit it for only a short period in the beginning. As we mature through these lessons, and life, we will visit it more frequently and stay a little longer before Mr. Ego brings us back to the 1% world. It is a process that requires vigilance. The more we practice, the better we get. Have fun watching your life become better and better each week as you practice the assignments.

These three phases of the Individuation Process provide a roadmap to follow as we navigate through our lives, making sense of where we are and where we are headed. It erases the fear of the unknown providing an understanding to our growth process, allowing us to feel more stable.

Here is a Preview of the Individuation Process:

Stage 1. *Disintegration:* Your old life becomes unraveled.

Stage 2. *Segregation:* Your family and friends become unraveled because you have changed and separate themselves from you, forcing you to find out who you really are if you are to emotionally survive their abandonment.

Stage 3: *Reintegration:* Once you knew who you are, you can knit yourself back together with 99% yarn into a happier, higher functioning, more peaceful person.

Disintegration begins when your life in this world of form begins to fall apart and no longer supports you. It often begins with a loss of your health, your money, the death of a loved one, a job, a religious belief, a marriage, or a combination of losses. The bad news is—it is terrifying. It hurts. Life seems such a struggle; it feels like you are trying to move uphill on a bicycle with square tires and it seems impossible to get life right.

Although difficult, the truth is, such losses are good news. This disintegration stage is essential. You can't put new wine in old bottles, lest it ruin the new wine. The disintegration process is designed to get rid of the old wine, or your own internal negative programming so you can replace it with healthy programming.

Assignment

Three days this week talk to a person you know who has lived through a tragedy and survived it well. Ask them if they think it made them a better person and how changed them. All week, ponder what they tell you

MIRACLE TIP | WEEK FORTY-TWO
THE SEGREGATION PROCESS

"Every time I thought I was being rejected from something good, I was actually being re-directed to something better."
(Steve Maraboli)

When someone segregates you, it doesn't mean anything is wrong with you. It simply means that person, or those persons, do not yet have the maturity to understand your value, what you may be going through, or what you have to offer. Because they don't know who they are, they can't see who you are. Often, they project their lack of love for themselves onto you, although, they are not conscious of their own feelings about themselves.

Yet, it is painful to be rejected, particularly by those you love. However, it is a valuable and necessary part of the Individuation process. It reminds you that you have, too often, allowed other people to define you. Then you allow their definitions to influence your own feelings about yourself . . . because you have not yet figured out who you truly are.

This segregation gives you incentive to truly figure out who you are . . . not a body, but a spirit . . . a spiritual offspring of our Creator with all the same potential as your parent. Jesus said you could do even greater things than he could do. (See John 14:12.)

What being segregated can do for you is what it did for me. It can push you to discover, for yourself, who you truly are and discover talents and powers you didn't know you had.

Since Jesus tells us we can do everything he has done and more and The Bible tells us Jesus and God are one . . . what does that say about you? Think on that!

So, this segregation (rejection) has redirected you to something much better. So, segregation is for you, a blessing.

Assignment

Read paragraph three above every day and ponder its profound meaning. Ask for spiritual help in getting this message from your head our head to your heart.

MIRACLE TIP | WEEK FORTY-THREE
THE REINTEGRATION PROCESS

"Wellness is the complete integration [Reintegration] of body, mind and spirit, the realization that anything we do, think, feel and believe has an effect on our state of well-being."
(Greg Anderson)

Reintegration is the final step in the Individuation process, the process of becoming spiritually and mentally healthy. Getting your head and heart working in harmony. It is a state of peace and well-being.

Review

Stage 1. *Disintegration:* Your old life becomes unraveled.

Stage 2. *Segregation:* Your family and friends become unraveled because you have changed and separate themselves from you. So you have to find out who you are. . . In Truth, you will find out you are so much more than you think you are.

Stage 3: *Reintegration:* Once you knew who you are, you can knit yourself back together with 99% yarn into a happier, higher functioning, more peaceful person.

Now you are knitting a new picture of your life using the new pieces of information and the new tools you have found. You are creating the stable life you desire using 99% thinking and actions; It is the only secure place to hang your hat. You know this because of your experience. The more you practice with these new tools the better your life gets.

Assignment

Decide what kind of life you really desire without concern for what anyone else thinks. Write a mission statement for yourself, and your family, if appropriate. Practice observing yourself, working towards having all your actions support your mission statement. Continue to refine your mission statement as you acquire more tools.

MIRACLE TIP | WEEK FORTY-FOUR

JUDGMENT, THE ROADBLOCK TO TRANSFORMATION

"Most of us are brought up in a home and school environment where emphasis was placed on constructive criticism, which actually is usually a disguise for faultfinding."
(Jerry Jampolsky, M.D., author of *Love is Letting Go of Fear*)

Why is judgment so damaging to our spiritual growth, or transformation? Because:

- Judgment puts us and others in fear—fear of not being okay.
- Fear separates is from our Creator.
- Judgment thwarts the process of transformation as transformation takes connecting to our maker.

Once you let go of the judgments creating fear, the truth of many repressed past experiences will begin to emerge for healing and "Ye shall know the truth and the Truth shall set you free" (**John 8:32**).

You now know it is a law of physics that like energies connect . . . which also makes it a law that unlike energies CANNOT connect. The Bible tells us God is love, an energy. Therefore, anyone in fear CANNOT connect to God, as fear is an unlike energy to love. If one can't connect to God, or their higher self, spiritual transformation is impossible.

And Christ told an inquiring Nicodemus that man must be born of the water and the spirit to enter into the kingdom of God. **Being born of the spirit is the transformation we have been discussing, the ticket into the Kingdom.**

Since nature does not tolerate a vacuum, once we get rid of the judgments, what do we replace them with? Look for the positive in every situation. In order to do this it helps to . . .

- Become the observer of self
- Notice when you are judging yourself or others
- Remember, being the judge is not who you are; you are offspring of the creator
- Remember, anyone not acting out of love is acting out of fear *and calling for love.*
- Remember perfect love casts out fear.

Now you will find: Being non-judgmental is much easier and much more fun, beneficial and rewarding . . . and the positive rewards are worth the effort.

Assignment

Each day this week observe your thoughts and behaviors that follow those thoughts. Anytime you find yourself judging or condemning yourself or anyone else, STOP and reread Miracle Tip Seventeen on Overcoming Reactive Behavior. Then ask your higher power to help make a genuine change in your thinking.

MIRACLE TIP | WEEK FORTY-FIVE

MORE ON LOVE
AND NON-JUDGMENT

*"When you look at a lamp, do you focus on the lampshade
or the light underneath? When you look at a person, do you
look for the light, or the body in which it resides? Always look
for the light, it is there. Love does not judge, it observes."*
(Claudia T. Nelson-Evans)

We have been programmed to find fault in ourselves and others and often
programmed to think that critical thinking is a virtue. Being critical is
not a virtue, except perhaps in academic research. We do need to evaluate
situations to see if it is in our highest and best interest to get involved . .
. yes evaluate, but not condemn.

There are two sides to everything as depicted by the yin/yang symbol in Lesson one. If we focus on the dark part, we only see dark, the negative in a person, or circumstance. If we focus on the light part, we will all see something positive in a person or circumstance.

How can we judge accurately? We can't. Just because a situation is not right for you, does not mean it is not right for someone else. If someone's behavior looks wrong, or 'bad' to us, we can't judge it, because we don't know the end result. It could be that the very situation we are judging as 'bad' could provide the very lessons to wake the person we are judging and change their life.

Focus on seeing the good, or potential good, in every situation. Work to stop judging people and situations. Good is there. In time you will find it is all good, even if that something seemed negative when it was happening. This principle as poignantly depicted in the following parable:

The Chinese Mare

A wise Chinese husband and father had few material goods in life, but he did have a wife and son he loved very dearly. And he had one mare in his barn. One day the mare got out. The neighbor cried, "Oh this is terrible, you've lost your only mare."

The wise Chinaman replied, "I don't know if this is good or bad, I just know I have lost my only mare."

The next day the mare returned with a whole herd of stallions. Again the neighbor cried, "Oh this is wonderful you have a whole herd of stallions."

Again the wise Chinaman said, "I don't know if this I good or bad, I just know I have a whole herd of stallions."

The next day the son tried to break a stallion got bucked off and broke his leg

Again the neighbor came over and said, "Oh this is terrible, terrible, your only son has broken his leg."

Again the wise Chinaman said, "I don't know if this I good or bad, I just know my son broke his leg."

The next day the recruiters from the Chinese infantry came to recruit the son to go to the front lines of the war where he would surely have been killed. But he couldn't go because . . . he had a broken leg.

Assignment

Write the following on a 3x5 card. Love does not judge. Love is humble; it simply observes and loves. Practice this all week and beyond.

MIRACLE TIP | WEEK FORTY-SIX

SEPARATING WANTS FROM DESIRES

"Desire is like the liquid of life that moves through the stem of the rose and allows the pedals to radiate with glorious color. When you block the flow of desire, the pedals cannot be nourished. Death begins to occur—death of the heart, death of the soul and lifelessness."
(*The Way of Mastery*)

Our desires are essential for our higher self to create anything. Our deepest desire is to love and be loved. So . . . up pops ego to divert us from using desire to create genuine love, programming us, with the help of the media, to dress up **wants** to make them look like real **desires**. The next trick ego plays is to make you **want things** like a better figure, the latest fashions, bigger homes, or the fanciest cars. . . things you think will bring you love, but can never bring genuine love.

Here is how to recognize the difference between wants and desires:

Wants

- Are fear-based and originate in our lower 1% thought system.
- Come from and/or cause feelings of lack, not feeling good enough, or not having enough.
- Come from our unconscious programming that we need material things to be loved.
- Come from our fears of emotional and/or physical survival.

Wants don't feel good. *Our feelings are always a barometer of which thought system we are in.*

Desires

We can recognize them when:

- They come from our 99% and are love based.
- They encourage us to understand that we are so much more than we think we are.
- They encourage us to face our fears.
- They encourage us to be kind, generous and forgiving.

Remember, while wants cause difficulty, they are not bad, as they often teach painful, but valuable, lessons that might have been learned in a less painful manner.

Assignment

Another week of self-examination. Take time to meditate on and distinguish between wants and true desires and understand it in your heart as well as your head.

LOVE IS OUR DEEPEST DESIRE

"Desire is everything."
(*The Way of Mastery*)

Everything is created through desire. Desire is not wrong. It is not to be judged, or feared. It is to be mastered, to be used to create in our 99% world. Everything is the effect of desire. It empowers you to create beautiful things full of beauty, power and miracles. It links you to the will of God.

Release any judgment about wants or desires.
All judgments come from our mis-programming.

Feel your feelings, all of your wants and all of your desires, and determine which come from the 1% and which come from the 99%. (Reread

Miracle Lesson 46, Separating Wants and Desires). Decide which you will act upon that will bring positive consequences.

None of your feelings are bad, They are never to be repressed. Neither is it wise to indulge them all. It is wise to make the choice to master them so they work in your best interest.

Desires coming from the 99% are always beneficial. Wants that come from the 1% are not bad, they are simply your teachers and sometimes teach difficult lessons.

Desire is the first step to creating anything. The rest of the formula follows. The DIAS formula it is a valuable key to connecting to our source. Apply it to creating more love in your life.

(D)esire to rid yourself to the blocks keeping you separated from your creator & the 99% world.

(I)ntend to do the fear erasing reprogramming that keeps you separated from yourself, and God. This takes discipline. (See Lesson 50.)

(A)llow your life to unfold. Don't try to force anything. Ignore the world telling you that you have to make all things happen.

(S)urrender everything to your higher power and patiently watch for miracles to happen.

Assignment

Since our greatest desire is love, Instead of striving so hard to get it, simply give it away every chance you get and use the DIAS formula above and notice what happens.

MIRACLE TIP | WEEK FORTY-EIGHT
WHY WE FEAR CHANGE

"It is not so much that we are afraid of change, or so in love with our old ways, But it's the place in between that we fear . . . it's like being between trapezes . . . There's nothing to hold on to."
(Marilyn Ferguson)

Change is difficult because we're giving up the known to face the fear of the unknown. We face fears such as:

- What will happen if I change?
- Can I survive, physically, emotionally, financially?
- Will my family, friends, boss, or my church still accept me?
- Am I strong enough to make needed changes?

The whole transition process is about facing our fears to connect to the love we are. Love and fear can't exist in the same person at the same time just as two objects can't occupy the same space at the same time, I continue to remind you.

Handling opposition in preparation for connecting to the 99% world of light requires change. You can do it and have done it, or you would not have gotten this far In *One-Minute Miracles*. And you will want to do more of it, as fear is the enemy of love.

Assignment

What fears are you willing to face to make needed change in your life? Think on this every day this week and come up with at least one change needed in your life and confront and heal the fear.

MIRACLE TIP | WEEK FORTY-NINE
HOW FEAR CRIPPLES US

"The only thing to fear is fear itself."
(Winston Churchill)

We must face change when life calls for it. Otherwise, we are like the caterpillar wrapped in a cocoon that has been placed into a mason jar . . . just as it was ready to change into a huge Polyphemus moth.

A very sad thing happens: The three-inch Mason Jar cannot accommodate the six-inch wingspan. The wings, unable to fully expand in the restrictive jar, harden in their crumpled state—producing a crippled moth.

Fear is your Mason jar crippling your growth,
expansion and transformation.

Nothing stands still. We can either choose to progress and change, or the law of entropy sets in and you retrogress; It is not possible to remain stationary in life and grow at the same time.

Assignment

Pat yourself on the back for overcoming your fears so far. Remember the Polyphemus moth and continue to walk through your fears. Fears aren't real; they are an illusion.

MIRACLE TIP | WEEK FIFTY
ERASING TAPES

"A person who wants to improve his/her health [physical or mental] has to change entire patterns of how he/she thinks. New patterns or attitudes will change his/her State of Being."
(Dr. Joe Dispenza)

Our minds work like computers—garbage in, garbage out.

Problem is, as I will again remind you, most of us have been programmed by well-meaning but often uninformed or misinformed parents, teachers, preachers and friends who were unknowingly programming those in their charge with garbage in programs, which are now creating garbage in those they pre-programmed.

This mis-programming, no matter how unintentional or well meant, often begins to manifest itself in dysfunctional behavior. The mis-programmer is not to blame. One is first mis-programmed himself and simply passes on the mis-programs, being unaware of what he/she is doing.

For example, the mother who criticizes her child's behavior, instead of showing the child the proper way to behave, thinking she is helping the child do better, is really damaging the child's self-esteem. But that is how she was raised, unaware of how her own child rearing damaged her.

Those programs, although damaging, likely worked for a time, but became the opposition because they were limiting. However, even the opposition can work to push you on to better things.

"There must be opposition in all things, otherwise righteousness could not be brought to pass." (2 Nephi)

Grade school learning is not bad, it is just limiting. You couldn't go on to high school without it. High school information is also limiting, and you can't go on to college without it.

So it is with all our experiences. In the end they are all good, even though some were limiting and/or painful. They all work to develop us into more loving individuals, if we choose such.

The good news is, these old dysfunctional programs can be erased and replaced with better information and experiences which we can use to create the life you now desire; to build the life you desire, you need the right tools. This book contains 52 unique tools that can help connect you to your real 99% self and own amazing creative powers.

As you come to recognize and erase your dysfunctional programs, those that create stress and unhappiness, and replace them with healthy programs, you will begin to connect with and creatively use your own creative 99% powers to create your own miracles. You will know you have functional programs by how you feel. Healthy programs bring peace, love, a feeling of well-being, and an ability to function well and create miracles.

Assignment

Take ten minutes out of each day to sit and ponder how all your experiences have been a blessing in some way and be grateful for them all. Then ponder your next steps.

MIRACLE TIP | WEEK FIFTY-ONE
SHED YOUR SKIN REGULARLY

*"If a snake were unable to cast off its old skin as it grows
it would strangle. If we are unable to cast off our old
too tight thoughts and beliefs as we grow, we strangle
our personal growth and transformation."*
(Claudia T. Nelson-Evans)

It is much easier for a snake to shed its skin than it is for a human to shed
old ideas and beliefs as humans have an ego. The snake just naturally
sheds its skin yearly to make room for new growth.

Our ego would have us hang onto judgments and old ideas for they
keep us in ego's territory, allowing ego to be in charge, keeping us from

growing. Ego loves control. It is job security for the ego. One of the ways ego keeps us in control is by creating and fanning our fears. When we conquer our fears, we conquer our ego. **Our ego is simply our fear thought system.**

With no ego working against us, we automatically tune into the love that we are and we are home again, transformed into a peaceful, happy, loving, well-adjusted, creative, highly functional individual.

Assignment

Go through the Table of Contents, place a star by those weeks that were most helpful and/or most challenging and visit them often to refresh your memory to keep you on the growth path.

MIRACLE TIP | WEEK FIFTY-TWO
BECOMING THE BUTTERFLY

the reason for the
JOURNEY!

"What the caterpillar calls the end of the world,
the master calls a butterfly."
(Richard Bach)

Bach sums up what we have been attempting to achieve with these Miracle Tips. We have been speaking of the death of our old thought system, feelings, actions and habits—the death of our old caterpillar self and the death of our negative, judgmental, self-critical nature.

The ego is like the caterpillar, in constant fear of survival, continually looking for its next leaf meal in order to survive. It can't see much further than the next leaf and has little desire to do so.

By contrast, the butterfly, like your 99% self is free. It can rise above the earth, enjoy a bigger life, experience the beauty that surrounds it as well as the tasty nectar from a variety of flowers.

The caterpillar is limited but the butterfly flies freely. However, between the caterpillar and the butterfly is the cocoon stage, the dark restrictive time which allows transformation to take place. In people life, it is called the Dark Night of the Soul. So, when you feel you are in a cocoon, going through the Dark Night, it is really the dark night of the ego, as it is dying. Remember, on the other side is the butterfly.

Remember: **If it had not been for the cocoon stage, the "Dark Night of the Soul" stage. You would never have become the butterfly.**

As you have now completed these lessons, you have broken out of your restrictive cocoon and you are now a butterfly. You are no longer a caterpillar creeping down a small branch looking for your next leaf meal.

Choose: *Will you use your wings to fly high and see wide and experience a world that you could never have experienced as a caterpillar?*

"What we achieve inwardly will change our outer world."
(Plutarch)

Assignment

Ponder the three stages of a butterfly. See it in your mind's eye, the slow caterpillar, the struggle to emerge from the cocoon, then the freedom of the butterfly. Consider the analogy and how it applies to your life.

CONCLUSION:
SECTION ONE, MIRACLES

N   ow we finish Bruce Lipton's sentence found in the introduction
and it won't surprise you because you have experienced it by
working this lessons.

You read in the introduction, the first half of Dr. Lipton's statement
as follows:

> **"You can create the world we want,**
> **and all we have to do is_____."**

Now we finish the statement:

"You can create the world we want, all we have to do is *become con-*
scious* and *then Heaven will be on this planet right now."

This entire book has been about becoming conscious.

This is a bold claim, but if you have faithfully done the assignments
suggested in each lesson, you have experienced the process of becom-

ing more conscious as you are experiencing your own life changing and becoming more like Heaven on earth.

Becoming conscious means you have become aware of the thoughts you have been thinking that have been creating the life you have been living, which have largely been based on limited information or misinformation and that your life has been largely built on illusions created by this misinformation. That is another bold statement, but remember, there is only 1% of truth found in this ego world where our minds generally hang out.

Webster's Universal Encyclopedic Dictionary defines **consciousness** as: "The quality or state of being aware, especially of something inside yourself."

Using this definition, **becoming conscious** would mean, for our purposes, to be the non-judgmental observer of our own behavior, noticing what is going on inside of you that produces peace and happiness and what is going on inside of you that produces its opposite. Then your journey begins to find out what it takes to move you from one place to the other, a journey on which you have already embarked.

Congratulations!

You are already finding answers. You now realize that the thinking and behavior patterns, behaviors that don't bring you happiness, emerge from the way you have been perceiving a situation and thinking about it.

The reason you have been perceiving (or believing) this way is because of the erroneous way you have been programmed to see things.

Remember lesson #4
Thinking—>Feeling——>Actions——>Results

These lessons have been all about targeting some of our mis-thinking and finding better ways of seeing things. Since we haven't been able to cover every thinking error and replace it with healthy thinking, you can now do it for yourself.

Our entire journey has been, and is, a journey to walk through our fears to the Love we are

> **"God hath not given us a spirit of fear but of power**
> **and of love, and of a sound mind"**
> **(2 Timothy 1:7).**

So, if you find yourself feeling a bit depressed:

1. Recognize that your feelings are your barometer to reveal what you are thinking
2. Ask yourself what you were thinking when you began to feel depressed or unhappy.
3. Ask yourself where these ideas may have originated and if they are valid. If you are depressed or not feeling unhappy, you know your thinking is not based on truth.

Did these depression causing ideas originate from your upbringing, your religious training, books you have read, or your own perceptions?

1. Ask yourself how you can see this differently and keep thinking of new ways to see it until you find one thought that feels good.
2. Replace the old thinking with your new healthier thinking.

For a continual journey in finding thoughts based on truth which bring you happiness and peace of mind, Join the "How can I see this differently" movement.

Do a google search to find the "How can I see this differently movement."

REMEMBER: WHEN YOU ARE
ENGAGED IN THIS WORK YOU
ARE PROVIDING A SPARK
OF LIGHT THAT HAS THE
POTENTIAL OF UPLIFTING
EVERY MIND ON THE PLANET
AND BEYOND BECAUSE . . .
ALL MINDS ARE CONNECTED
AT A QUANTUM LEVEL.

AND WE WILL NEVER HAVE A PEACEFUL WORLD UNTIL WE HAVE PEACEFUL PEOPLE, AS PEOPLE ARE WHAT MAKE UP OUR WORLD.

WHEN THE POWER OF LOVE
OVERCOMES THE LOVE OF
POWER, THE WORLD WILL
KNOW PEACE. (JIMI HENDRIX)

SECTION TWO:
TRUE INSPIRATIONAL STORIES

Section Two contains stories that show the miracles that happen when one's thinking has been transformed from 1% thinking to 99% thinking. The following stories reveal the more dramatic results of this transformation.

Most of the benefits that those new to this work will be experiencing are the miracles of improved relationships and greater peace of mind. But if you continue on this path, the dramatic results experienced by those in the stories can become common place in your life.

I'M GETTING BETTER EVERY DAY

Have you ever spent a great deal of time studying something and wondering why you spent so much time at it, as it didn't seem to add anything to your present life? Then you realize, when the future enters your life as the new present, there was a reason for your obsession?

I was a stay-at-home mom with eight children struggling to squeeze all I had to do into the limited time I had in which to accomplish it. Still I was obsessed with the mind and how it worked. I still wonder how I found time to squeeze the study into my schedule. But I did. Now I know why and you will too after you read my story.

In spite of all my study, it was my mother who taught me more about the mind than any book could . . . in a very dramatic and painful manner.

The story begins with the shock of an emergency phone call from Michelle, our baby sitter, when we were in Taiwan. In her broken English she muttered, "Your mother in hospital, has 'bruise in lung' mus come home."

My husband, being an M.D. knows a bruised lung is not an emergency and getting out of Taiwan during the Chinese New Year would be very difficult. The more he tried to explain this the more insistent Michelle became . . . Mus come home, mus come home!

Finally realizing she was either intentionally withholding information, which did not sound good, or she did not have the vocabulary to fully explain the situation, we knew we had better get home. After explaining the situation to the airlines, they granted us passage home.

Two days later we landed on American soil in Salt Lake City, grabbed a cab and headed for the Utah Valley Hospital in Provo, Utah.

My first shock was to find Mother in an Intensive care unit. The next shock was to walk into what was supposed to be her room and find a woman with a swollen head, massively bruised face and a black and purple neck, results of blood draining from the head injury. I was shocked.

"We are in the wrong room," I said to my husband and headed back to tell the nurse she had given us the wrong unit number.

He grabbed my hand and pulled me back into the room, pulled me to this poor woman's bedside and pushed up her upper lip to show me her teeth and said, "This is your mother."

I felt dizzy and disoriented and sat down before I fell. Those were my mother's teeth.

My mother and her husband had been driving through Spanish Fork Canyon pulling a motor home on their way to Texas for the winter when a Cement truck, going far too fast for the icy roads, hit black ice, rolled over their vehicle and crushed them.

While sitting beside my mother, still in a disoriented state of mind, a nurse walked in and in a very detached manner said, "She has brain stem injury. She has a 5% chance of living, and if she does live, she will be a vegetable."

That night I slept a few fitful hours and said to myself, "Death I can handle; it might be a blessing in her condition." But mother was a strong-willed woman who had the heart of a forty-year-old, vegetable was the more likely of the two options.

But vegetable was not acceptable . . . not acceptable . . . not acceptable. How many times did I say that to myself? I don't remember. Suddenly, I began to understand why I had been so interested in how the mind works. Spirit knows the future and knew there would be a time when I would need this knowledge to prevent my mother from living a half-life trapped in her body and unknown to me, inspired me to study the mind in preparation for helping my mother. I used that knowledge to devise a plan preventing my mother from living a half-life trapped in her own body.

I knew the subconscious mind (the 99% mind) had the power to heal the body and much more. Yet, I also knew it was difficult to access because the conscious mind (the 1% mind) continually got in the way being programmed to believe, as the nurse did, she would likely not recover, or would be a vegetable.

But now her conscious ego mind was asleep, it couldn't interfere. I began working with her subconscious mind. Every day for three months while she was in the hospital I would go in and say, "Mother, you are getting better every day." I would say it at least one hundred times every day.

After three months the hospital sent her to a nursing home to die. Every day for another month I visited my mother and continued the routine, one hundred times a day, saying, "Mother, you're getting better every day."

I walked into the nursing home one day after she had been there for a month just as the nurse came rushing out of her room wide eyed and speechless as if she had seen a ghost. I tried to prepare myself for what I might see when I entered Mother's room. Finally, the nurse found her composure and spoke.

"Every day when I go in to care for Beth, I walk in and say, "Well how are you doing today, Beth?"

Of course, I know she is in a coma . . . ***But today she said, "I'm getting better every day."*** Those were the exact words I'd spoken to her thousands of times. She even spoke in the same tone of voice I had used to program her mind to heal.

She did get better every day until that stopped and we realized why. Her well-meaning, but ill-informed friends and relatives thinking with their ego minds, began arriving and we found out they were saying things like, "Beth, I just can't believe this, people don't recover from brain stem injury."

While I had always believed in the power of the subconscious mind, now I knew for certain of its power, and have continued to study and learn about it and use it to heal my own traumatic life.

Now, I offer all I have learned to you with proof it works, provided by my mother. That 99% mind contains all power and all knowledge and is worth the effort to reconnect to it.

THE UNUSUAL PHARMACY

David was distraught. Up until now his life had been easy. Being the son of a very rich business man, he was raised with every physical thing he wanted or needed. Yet he was deprived of the love and affection of a healthy mother. Therefore, he was raised with some things he didn't want, like a Nanny.

He dealt with his lack of motherly love and affection because of everything else he had been given until . . . his father had a business reversal and the money was gone. It was more than he could deal with. He was still living at home at age twenty supported by Dad. Not knowing how to live in the world and make it on his own, he turned to drugs to salve the fear and pain, became severely addicted, and eventually became suicidal.

He was a bright boy and desperately wanted help. He had tried several therapists to no avail. But still he had the burning desire to rid himself of this terrible addiction he had created. Then one afternoon he was riding his motorcycle down the streets of San Francisco past a pharmacy that created custom medications.

On a whim he decided to stop in at this pharmacy having nothing in particular to purchase. He began browsing around and it surprised him to see the pharmacy had a few books for sale.

He picked up a book that looked like it would help him tremendously and purchased it. After reading the book he found the author was a local author.

He took the book to a friend to show her what he had found and how much he loved it, casually asking her if she happened to know the author.

"Know him . . . I work for him," she said.

"Do you think he would see me as a client?"

The author consented to see him and he is now happy, well-adjusted and financially successful.

That is only half of the story. The author of that book has his own story of how that book came to be on that pharmacy shelf.

One day the author stopped to pick up a compounded prescription and while walking in the door he got this strange message. "Ask the owner if he would like to carry your book in his pharmacy."

"This is a pharmacy, not a book store," the author responded tacitly. Again, the message came, "Ask the owner if he would like to carry your book in his pharmacy."

The author wanted to respond as before but stopped himself and thought, "Well the worst thing that can happen is he will say 'no' and I will just feel stupid for having asked." But, he realized that would just be his ego talking trying to make him feel stupid.

He continued his conversation with himself. Since he was practicing not listening to his ego and not letting it run his life, he decided to ask.

The pharmacy owner was very gracious explaining he liked supporting local artists and put several books on the shelf.

Because the pharmacist, the author and the young man struggling with addiction all listened to their 99% voice, a life was saved. And a fellow human being was made whole. What would have happened to this young man if he, the author or the pharmacist had listened to the ego, their 1% mind instead of their 99% mind?

DOWN AND OUT TO UP, UP, UP

oger's life sucked. He had just gone through a difficult divorce, in which he lost everything. He was out of a job, out of money and his future looked bleak. He heard about a possible job and traveled a long distance to see if he could land that job. He'd been a drifter and had no real goals in life. The only option he had for any viable existence was this job; and it was a long shot.

He could have been the poster child for one experiencing the first step of Dr. Carl Jung's Individuation Process . . . It seemed everything in his life had *disintegrated . . . no wife, no life, no money, no job and no certain job prospects.*

When he arrived at his destination, they did offer him the job, but it wasn't yet ready for him to start. He had barely enough money to stay in a cheap motel for two weeks and a tank of gas to get out of town. If the job didn't materialize within that two week period, he would have to leave, although he had no idea where he would go.

Having two weeks to kill he walked to a nearby bookstore and thought he would buy a book he'd heard about called *A Course in Miracles.* He would need a miracle if this job didn't pan out. Roger had also heard they had "Course in Miracles" study groups and asked the store owner if she knew of a group in town.

"Sure do, we are having a class here tonight," she said. When Roger walked into the classroom that evening, a man sitting in the back of the room said, "Where have you been, we have been waiting for you?"

Roger had never seen this man before and was startled by his inquiry and just stared at him in amazement, but for some reason didn't ask questions. This man's name was Christian and they became friends.

Hanging out with Christian was a real trip for Roger. Christian had a van he lived in and traveled from place to place. He didn't have a job, nor any prospects for one, nor did he seem to care, for he always had the money he needed. Roger had story after story he told about the unusual experiences he had with Christian.

One of the most miraculous was at a restaurant. Christian ordered crab legs. He'd eat one plate full and the plate would fill up again. That happened several times and a when it was time to go the plate filled up again and he put it in a to-go box and took it home.

As Roger shared his experience with me I asked, "Didn't you ask Christian how in the world he could do that?"

"No," Roger replied simply, without further explanation.

I was left to wonder why he hadn't questioned him. Perhaps it was because he didn't expect to receive an answer, at least a logical one, or maybe it was just too sacred of an experience to question. After the night at the restaurant Christian said goodbye to the study group and drove off to who knows where.

In addition to Roger's amazing experiences with Christian, there is an even more amazing story of what happened to him as he read and experienced the life changing principles in *A Course in Miracles*. Roger read it for several hours a day, being alone in his room for those two weeks. He had revelation after revelation, being amazed at how it validated some of his own thinking and beliefs, which his family and friends didn't understand or accept. Roger experienced an entire transformation of spirit and felt whole and at peace for the first time in his life.

Now the two weeks were up and the job had not materialized so Roger had to leave. He was getting packed to leave when the call came. The voice on the other end said, "Your job is ready."

Roger did a remarkable job for this company. His reputation spread and he became known as the acoustic ceiling guru in the commercial building world and he never wanted for work again.

Roger credited his success to the spiritual transformation he experienced while sitting alone in his motel room for two weeks reading *A Course in Miracles* in which his whole way of thinking and feeling changed. Now seeing life differently, his actions changed. Because his actions changed so did the results he experienced. And as you can see after reading his story, they changed in a very positive way.

Roger knew the job being delayed was no accident. It gave him time to read and experience the transformation, the process by which he became emotionally and spiritually healthy. It began with his life disintegrating and humbling him.

He realized his life had been perfect. Had it not "sucked" his whole transformation could not have occurred. Roger knew it all was a "God thing."

While Roger's experience is inspirational, it is also unique. For most people this transformational process is more gradual.

For additional inspirational stories of what can happen when one moves from 1% thinking to 99% thinking, read *Rising from Ashes: Discover your Hidden Power Through Adversity* by Claudia T. Nelson

SECTION THREE:
UNDERSTANDING THE TRANSFORMATION PROCESS

This section is taken from my book "Murder, Death and Rebirth written in 2012 and revised and updated for *One-Minute Miracles* It explains the transformation process from several perspectives.

THE TRANSFORMATION PROCESS

After studying a bit about wave physics and Einstein's theory of relativity, I discovered Einstein knew something about transformation.

And through Native Americans and other indigenous groups, with Shamans as their spiritual leaders, I learned that they express this transformation process as a Shamanistic Journey.

To make this transformational process even more clear, I have drawn from another source. Studying how a silk worm transforms into a butterfly, I recognized it was a wonderful analogy to explain how to turn difficulty and limitation into transformation.

Pulling together what the silk worm, Einstein, and the Shamans have to teach gives a more understandable picture of this transformational process.

Next, I'll add depth to the process with an experience I had with my son, Jon on the Road to Iosepa.

I am sharing several examples of how transformation occurs knowing that the better one understands the transformational process, the less daunting it seems. Using analogies, or something we can understand, to explain something that is difficult to understand is the value of analogy. Understanding transformation from this perspective you can then simply see it is a magnificent growth process and be grateful for it.

First the silk worm analogy:

The Silk Worm

Most of us have seen a caterpillar slowly inching its way along a tree branch concerned about only one thing—survival. The caterpillar's great goal in life is to find its next leafy meal.

Contrast that with the butterfly it is destined to become. The butterfly is free to fly high and see wide, to experience the feel of a flower under its feet, to taste the sweetness the nectar provides, to fly from flower to flower, from bush to bush, and beyond.

Which would you rather be? Few would choose the caterpillar.

Research done by Harvard Zoology Professor Carl Milton Williams, reveals the secret of this transformation and what happens inside the cocoon. Something similar happens to humans who desire a butterfly life.

The First Stage

Professor Williams explains that scattered through the mushy tissues of the big green caterpillars are a small group of cells called Imaginal Discs that lie dormant while the caterpillar is growing. These cells contain the blueprint for the butterfly. When the caterpillar has grown as large as it can, its tissues begin to break down and form a yolky fluid.

When we as humans have grown psychologically and spiritually as large as we can, our lives begin to break down. We may lose a job, a spouse a loved one, our possessions, or our philosophy of life that has sustained us. This wakes up our Imaginal thinking as we, like the butterfly, begin to transform into something better. It is interesting to note that this transformation begins in the brain in both the caterpillar and the human.

The Second Stage

What occurs before a caterpillar becomes a butterfly is the cocoon stage. It is a dark and restrictive place, but a necessary one. You can't get from caterpillar to butterfly without going through the cocoon stage. So it is with humans.

As the dissolving of the caterpillar begins, it encases itself in the dark restrictive pupa. Here it continues to dissolve, creating cytochrome enzymes which provide food for the Imaginal Cells to feed upon, multiply and become a butterfly. These cytochrome enzymes are also found in humans.

This dark, seemingly restrictive place in humans, called the pupa when speaking of a caterpillar transforming into a butterfly, is often called "The Dark Night of the Soul when speaking of human transformation. Opposition dissolves our old thinking into the food our awakened Imaginal thoughts feed upon as they grow and multiply until our thoughts are transformed. (See Miracle Tip 42)

The Third Stage

Although the caterpillar was born for the purpose of becoming a butterfly, as this transformation takes place, its immune system recognizes these Imaginal Disc cells as foreign and tries to destroy them, just as our own fear-based ego acts as its own immune system trying to stop our transformational process.

But the Imaginal Discs in the caterpillar are feeding on good food, multiplying rapidly, *linking up* and gaining strength, causing the immune system to break down, allowing this transformation to the place.

Linking Up

It is because these Imaginal Cells link themselves to each other that they gain the strength to overcome the immune system, which is trying to destroy them.

For us to gain the strength to break down the ego rather than having it overcome us, we can learn from the Imaginal Cells. We can link ourselves to others who use and encourage higher thinking. There is strength in numbers. Consider maintaining your link to your OMM study group.

As humans we need to link up with like-minded people to keep our ego immune system from destroying our transformational process

As we continue to develop our higher thought system, we need to feed it higher level everything . . . higher thoughts, books, magazines, movies, conversation, activities, *and associates.*. That helps our higher thought system which is growing rapidly, continue to grow. Eventually it will be strong enough to control the old ego—the "What's-in-it-for-me" thought system.

This research provides us with a beautiful analogy of what happens as we transform from victim to victor thinking. Untransformed we're a caterpillar largely concerned only with survival. Transformed we are free. We see an amazing view of ourselves and life we've never seen before. What happens in the cocoon to allow that to happen is most instructive as we apply it to Human transformation.

Einstein's View of Transformation

Einstein gave us a formula for personal transformation. Although most people see it as only a wisdom quote, it is so much more. He adds an additional dimension to the transformation process by helping us recognize our two thought systems and how they work.

Einstein's Transformational Formula

> *"You can't solve the significant problems you face at the same level of thinking you were at when you created them."*
> **(Albert Einstein, See Miracle Tips 41 and 43)**

It sounds simple enough. But as you ponder this idea of two levels of thinking, you come to understand how deeply and profoundly brilliant this statement is and what it implies.

Again we discuss Einstein's two levels of thinking. You will recall there is one level where we create our problems —that's Level One (The Ego level), also known was 1% thinking, for it is where you find only 1% of truth. It is the place where we create our problems. Then there is Level Two (The Imaginal Level) also known as 99% thinking, for it is the place we find 99% of Truth, Truth with a capitol T. This is the thinking place where we solve our problems. Yet most people don't understand we have two thought systems, nor do they know each thought system has its own agenda, a will and a voice of its own.

Even if they understood, they wouldn't know how to get from one level to the other. So they keep trying to solve their problems at the same level of thinking they were at when the created them the place they can't be solved, just as Einstein explained. Neither True problem-solving nor transformation can take place with level one thinking, so we stay trapped as a victim in the ego world of fear.

To review how these two levels of thinking work go back to Miracle Tip 45 and reread the story of the Chinese Mare. Contrasting the thinking of the Chinaman and that of his neighbor will help you better understand the difference between these two levels of thinking. Then read it again after we discuss transformation from two additional points of view, that of the Shaman and that of my son.

The Shaman's Visual View of Transformation

The Shaman also explains the transformational journey in a slightly different three-stage process, the underworld, the upper world and the middle world. The underworld stage is equivalent to Jung's Disintegration stage. The upper world stage is equivalent to Jung's Reintegration stage. The middle world stage explains what you do after you have been transformed.

Discovering Shamanism clarified the stages of transformation I experienced. We come into this world to experience duality, meaning the light and the darkness, good and evil, etc. We need this duality until we've learned the lessons it teaches. The lessons are explained in this three-step process we are now calling the Shamanistic Journey.

All of us at one time or another will have to face darkness in our lives. It comes at different times and in different ways, but no one gets through this journey without experiencing darkness to some degree. Its purpose is to humble us and make us realize that all we thought we knew about life was mostly illusion for we were thinking with the wrong thought system.

What we thought was truth while vibrating at lower level frequencies, now comes under question as we begin to discover our own truth rather than living by someone else's. But what else could we expect. As we have noted, those who passed their illusions, or misinformation, onto us had the same information passed on to them.

So the illusions and misinformation keep getting passed around for generations until someone becomes the transition person for a family who has the courage to take this Shamanistic Journey. This family transition person generally becomes such as their own life is breaking down, forcing them to confront the illusions and replace them with Truth, or at least a much higher perspective.

Before we can correct these misperceptions, we must face our old limiting belief system and recognize it is time to move beyond it. This is the part of our Shamanistic Journey usually referred to as "The Dark Night of the Soul." Native Americans refer to it as the underworld phase.

The Underworld

Again, our Shamanistic Journey begins with some major part of our old life falling apart. We may lose a loved one, a job, our money, our health, or a belief system. This is a clue it's time for your journey to begin. This yarn and beeswax Huichol art piece explains what the first stage of our journey feels like.

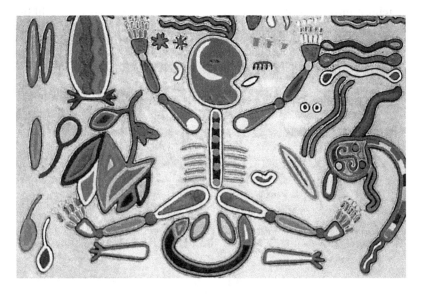

When we understand what is happening and know it is temporary, and understand that we'll be put back together in a better manner than before, our fear is greatly reduced. Before this can happen, we must become humble and teachable, willing to see things differently. That is the purpose of this Underworld stage of growth. When we are humbled and willing to see things differently, we are ready to move on to the upper world.

The Upper World

This image depicts an individual who has been through the Underworld experience and has been humbled sufficiently to be taken to the upper world to be taught higher truths. You will note that the eagle is picking the person up by their feet, symbolizing humility. You will also note that this man is dressed in black. Black is traditionally the color worn when going to the funeral of one who has died, symbolizing the man's pride has died. Now he can be reborn. Think again about Christ's conversation with Nicodemus about having to be born again, or reborn of the water and the spirit, to enter into the kingdom? Now, humbled, he can be reborn into this upper world (Kingdom) experience where he will be taught to think differently.

The Middle World

In the third part of the Shamanistic Journey, you come back awakened and enlightened, ready to teach what you have learned. (Eyes to see, active imagination art by Claudia T. Nelson).

The middle world is where most of humanity hangs out living lives of quiet desperation, waiting for you. Being transformed you'll be anxious to share what you learned in the Upper World with those you have been commissioned to teach. They will be those who can learn best from your teaching style, which matches their learning style. They will be those who have been humbled and are ready to listen. They will show up in your life, be it one or many, for you now have eyes that see with wisdom and love.

That is all there is to it, the Shamanistic explanation of the three-step process of transformation shared here to save you many hours of grief as you have occasion to make sense of a life that is making no sense.

Perfect love swallows up fear just as light swallows up darkness, and all that is left is love.. This knowledge can help you fulfill your destiny.

> **_Man's unfulfilled destiny is the shame of the universe._**
> **(_Journey to Promethea,_ the movie)**

The truth is transformation is a glorious process. It means you have grown to the point where you are ready to be transformed. Analyzing the transformational process from the silkworm's, Einstein's and the Shaman's perspectives, we know what to expect on the journey and have been provided the tools to make the transformation successful.

For those who still consider this a frightening time, it's only because of the belief system that is afraid of change. It's your Level One fear-based thinking.

You can stay out of fear by using the following peace-creating mantra: **I am gaining more and more peace and happiness as I surrender to this transformational process.**

Know that all you are going through is for your good. *Accept* that the outcome is for your good. *Explore* new ideas . . . as we are about to do on the . . .

Road to Iosepa

A road trip with my son helped me further understand why sharing (a form of giving) is so valuable. This story reveals an essential internal change that occurs during a Shamanistic Journey—It reveals why giving is the only True and permanent way to get for yourself. When You give what you have, money, time or talents, miraculously you get what you need. My son, Jon, gave me a beautiful analogy to explain this truth as we traveled the Road to Iosepa together.

It was a Saturday morning in October 2006 after we'd buried Grandma Goates. It was the first time the entire family had been together for over seven years; it called for a celebration. Fourteen members of my family headed east toward Grantsville, Utah, to the remote ghost town of Iosepa.

My son, Byron, shared the history of Iosepa. He explained that in the early 1900s, a group of Hawaiians, who had responded to the message of the Mormon missionaries came to Utah to be by a temple and settled near Grantsville, in a place they called Iosepa. Tragedy struck when a fire started in one house in Iosepa. Because the homes were built very close together, all the homes burned in succession.

After their homes were gone, there was nothing to tie them to Utah. Since their church had built a temple in Hawaii, they decided to return to their native home. Some surviving members of those who died in Iosepa returned there once a year on Memorial Day to Honor their dead by placing one flower on each individual grave.

When we arrived that October, most of the flowers from the Hawaiians' latest Memorial Day trip had dried up. Yet one lone flower on one long grave still looked fresh. I was certain it contained seeds of a touching story.

The Hawaiians left little behind except for a small monument and pavilion at the East end of the fended-in grave yard telling the story of this forgotten community. The graveyard gate was marked on one side by a unique-looking metal mosquito attached to a pole on one side of it. It looked like it had been carved with a blowtorch from a thin sheet of metal. A rabbit attached to the adjacent pole on the other side of the gate appeared to have been carved from the same piece of metal with the same torch.

The graveyard, pavilion, mosquitos and jackrabbits are the sole remains of this community, except for some wonderful rolling hills, perfect for four-wheeling and that is why we were there. The graveyard was symbolic for me as our trip allowed me to bury my doubts about something I had been pondering for some time which had to do with the value of giving. It was a conversation with my son, Jon, on the way to Iosepa that concluded my thinking about giving and its value.

It was our conversation about color that provided a brilliant analogy, clarifying the thinking I had been doing on this universal law of giving and its value. I don't even know what brought up our conversation about color. Sometimes, 99% thoughts pop into my head, and I said, "Jon, I've read that white is a combination of all colors. Then I had an artist tell me if you mixed all colors together, you'd have black. You're an artist; can you clarify this for me?" He hesitated for a moment and then said:

> "Let's think about color another way. You have to realize that nothing we are looking at really has any color. The color comes from the light that reflects off the objects we see."

"Then why isn't everything the same color," I asked? I continued, "The light is shining the same on everything we are seeing. Yet those bushes on the right are a combination of greens and the road is black—why is that?"

"Light has the full spectrum of colors and the colors we see on any given object are determined by which rays the object is reflecting back. If it is reflecting back the green rays, you have a green object," Jon explained.

I continued to question, "What about the black road? It has no color. Does that mean it is reflecting nothing back?"

"That is exactly what but means," Jon said.

My question had been answered—all colors combined are both black and white. Which form it takes is determined by whether the object receiving the light, reflects (gives) it back or hoards it.

If all the light rays received from the sun are reflected (given) back it would create white. If none of them were given back, it would create black. That pretty much sums up our lower-level and higher-level thinking.

When we give some, we get more back. But often we give out of obligation, being afraid we will be condemned if we don't, or will feel guilty if we don't. That is fear-based energy and does not bring the best results. When we give, even though we fear we don't have enough, we are giving out of obligation or guilt. This only adds low-level fear energy to the equation and rarely brings positive results.

If we want to receive more, we need to give more; and we need to give out of love, not from feelings of lack or fear.

***Giving with the right energy
is a transformational experience.***

I SEND YOU LOVE,
PEACE AND BLESSINGS.

AND AS THEY SAY IN *STAR WARS*,
MAY THE FORCE BE WITH YOU!

ACKNOWLEDGMENTS

Thanks to the late Jerry Jampolski, M.D. and his wife, Dr. Diane Cirincione, for generously allowing me to use art from Jerry's best-selling book, *Love Is Letting Go of Fear,* to illustrate and enhance each week's lesson.

Thanks to the late Ronald Lee Brown for believing in my work and generously supporting it.

Thanks to all of my Monday Morning Tip blog readers from around the world who sent thousands of emails thanking me and letting me know how much the information in the blog changed their lives, stimulating me to get it all into this book, as the MMT blog is no longer available.

Thanks to all of my colleagues who gave such beautiful endorsements in my book, *Rising From Ashes,* and who still encourage and support my work.

And I must acknowledge my artists again. They are so fabulous.

Thanks to my good friend and artist, Stephanie Mullani, for going the extra mile doing and redoing art images until my major concepts were well-illustrated. Thanks to B. Smith for taking time from his busy schedule to use his artistic talents to create some of the interesting and creative art concepts in this book.

Finally, thanks to my Morgan James Publishing family who have also gone the extra mile and been so patient in getting this book into your hands.

Founder David. Hancock
My editors:
    Valerie Cassidy
    Karla Briggs
    Cortney Donelson
Morgan James support team:
    Naomi Chellis and the other team members:
Amber, Jessica, Lauren, and Jodi
    Shannon Peters
    Jim Howard, Branding
Web Design and promotion:
    Bertha Edington

ADDITIONAL RESOURCES

"Nothing real can be threatened;
Nothing unreal exists.
Herein lies the peace of God."
The Way of Mastery published by the Shanti Christo Foundation and
A Course in Miracles published by the Foundation for Inner Peace

For a continued and deeper study on this spiritual transformation process, I recommend two books as resources, A *Course in Miracles* and *The Way of Mastery*. They would be great resources to continue this study with your group.

Also, I have a monthly blog post that may interest you. Readers are asked to send in their stories about how any of the lessons in this book changed their life. I will select and publish one story each month on the website and offer a ten- to fifteen-minute free consultation to those who are published. Good luck!

ABOUT THE AUTHOR

C laudia T. Nelson has a B.A. in Writing and Literature, with minors in Psychology and Art and an additional degree in Communication. She has conducted successful seminars on personal empowerment, transformation, and marriage relationships since 2012. Her writing career began in the 1970s, when her first psychological/spiritual personal empowerment article was published in *Ensign* magazine in several different languages, with worldwide distribution. Prior to writing *One-Minute Miracles*, Claudia published several pieces, including *Rising from Ashes: Discover Your Hidden Power through Adversity*, which is an empowering resource that shares her story of courage, resilience, and rebirth. She also wrote the successful blog "Monday Morning Tips" and has appeared on PBS, CBS, and NBC TV stations as well as been featured in *Forbes* magazine. There is no doubt, adversity has shaped Claudia's life. And through it, she realized her choices about how to respond to adversity—not living as a victim made all the difference. Claudia currently resides in Boise, Idaho.

APPENDIX

SUGGESTED MEDITATION

I F YOU DO NOT HAVE A FAVORITE MEDITATION, I SUG-
GEST THIS ONE.

It is simple to do and you will immediately feel the difference
between being in the 1% world of fear and the 99% world of love.

Step 1. Sit in a comfortable chair with your feet touching the ground,
legs uncrossed, and hands in your lap with palms up.

Step 2. Relax every part of your body beginning with your feet. You
may actually feel like you have become part of the chair.

Step 3. Take three deep breaths and let them out slowly.

Step 4. As you inhale visualize the word PEACE hanging in the air
in front of you. Now as you breath in, breath in that word PEACE right
into your nostrils and watch it, AND FEEL IT go down your throat
into the lungs into the blood stream moving through every organ in
your body.

Step 5. As you exhale visualize the word STRESS or FEAR coming
out your nostrils and crumbling to the ground as you exhale. Notice how
you FEEL.

Step 6. If unwanted thoughts keep appearing just notice them and go back to your breathing. In the beginning your 1% mind will fight you on this meditation, but keeping at it will pay huge dividends.

Step 7. Continue breathing in PEACE and breathing out fear, up to twenty minutes twice a day or more. If you are not accustomed to meditating, begin with five minutes per day and work your way up to twenty minutes or more twice a day. Notice how you feel.

Once you become comfortable with the meditation and feel your energy has moved into the 99% world, you can begin asking questions. Be patient and wait. The answer may come while you are meditating, or it may come at a much unexpected time when your mind is calm, like when you are taking a shower or chopping vegetables. If you are having a difficult time finding a calm mind, watch for answers to come through an unsuspecting friend or relative who may say something they don't even realize is an answer to your question.

Some of you will have fast results with the meditation process and for others it may take months to really connect. Keep at it; don't be discouraged. It took the famous Ester Hicks' nine months of meditation before she connected to her guide(s) Abraham. Many of you know Abraham-Hicks who has become famous for all the wise answers she gets for herself and others.

A free ebook edition is available with the purchase of this book.

To claim your free ebook edition:

1. Visit MorganJamesBOGO.com
2. Sign your name CLEARLY in the space
3. Complete the form and submit a photo of the entire copyright page
4. You or your friend can download the ebook to your preferred device

Print & Digital Together Forever.

Snap a photo

Free ebook

Read anywhere

Printed in the USA
CPSIA information can be obtained
at www.ICGtesting.com
JSHW082042040923
47807JS00004B/44

9 781636 980843